"Pastor Jonathan Dodson poignantly unpacks the perennial truths of the greatest sermon of all time, revealing its ancient wisdom for our morally confused times. Replete with real-world examples, both historical and contemporary, this book offers a compelling countercultural solution to our moral crisis grounded in Jesus' upside-down kingdom."

Allen Yeh, associate professor of intercultural studⁱ Biola University

"Jonathan has written an impo.   vided and hostile culture. Brimming   e, and a beautiful way forward for the: this book will greatly improve our credibility as   world."

Jon Tyson, lead pastor at Church of the City New York, author of *The Burden Is Light*

"The Beatitudes can be intimidating to Christians, and more so the more we know what they mean. This book provides fresh and honest insight into the beauty and glory of these words of the kingdom. Whatever crisis you may face now or in the future, I pray this book will reframe for you what it means to be 'blessed.'"

Russell Moore, president, The Ethics & Religious Liberty Commission of the Southern Baptist Convention

"I can't think of a more encouraging and challenging way to spend our time than to dwell on these famous words of Jesus. Jonathan Dodson will help you understand their revolutionary meaning and also apply Jesus' teaching for our cultural moment."

Collin Hansen, editorial director of The Gospel Coalition, author of *Blind Spots: Becoming a Courageous, Compassionate, and Commissioned Church*

"*Our Good Crisis* is a compass, drawing the reader back to our true north, to God himself. As we walk across the ever-changing landscape of our age, Dodson reminds us of the never-changing goodness of the Beatitudes. God in heaven is the source of virtue, of all that's good, of the very remedy needed for the crises we see in the world and in ourselves. This meditation on the Beatitudes will nourish your soul and exhort you to walk with Jesus, living out his kingdom here on earth, by the power of his Spirit."

Jen Oshman, author of *Enough About Me: Find Lasting Joy in the Age of Self*

"*Our Good Crisis* is exactly the kind of Christian book we need more of—one that examines the text of Scripture carefully while listening to the anxieties of our age with sympathy. By applying this approach to the Beatitudes, the opening lines of the Sermon on the Mount, Jonathan Dodson achieves something wonderful. He encourages believers to live faithfully amid our moral and technological complexities, and he helps doubters imagine what it would be like to take Christ's ancient wisdom seriously today."

John Dickson, author and historian, senior lecturer in public Christianity, Ridley College, Melbourne, Australia

"A keen look beneath the frenzied surface of our modern world to see what lurks there—how people think, both about themselves and their world. It is these attitudes that are here brought face-to-face with the truth of the Beatitudes. This book is direct and helpful."

David F. Wells, Distinguished Senior Research Professor, Gordon-Conwell Theological Seminary

"Reflecting on secular and nonsecular thinkers, Jonathan does an amazing job of pointing us to the message that brings about true human flourishing. This book will challenge and encourage you to boldly live out your faith. This is a must read!"

Ivan Valdez, member at City Life Church, Austin

"It's easy enough to see the impending crises brought about by our technical, data-driven age; it's harder to believe that these difficulties present us with an opportunity for self-reflection, and yes, even spiritual growth. In *Our Good Crisis*, Jonathan K. Dodson guides us back to the ancient wisdom of the Sermon on the Mount, showing readers how the Beatitudes can lead us to blessing even in—especially in—the modern age. Confronting everything from our propensity to outrage to our fixation with self to our comfort addictions, *Our Good Crisis* reveals Jesus' words to be as good news to us today as they were to those who first heard them."

Hannah Anderson, author of *All That's Good: Recovering the Lost Art of Discernment*

"We are in an age where the performance of the self is more important than the reality of the self, creating what Dodson calls a crisis of the good. Jesus' words, then, in Matthew 5 can feel alien to us—otherworldly. They demand that the inner self be the chief concern, rather than how the world sees us. Near the end of his book Jonathan Dodson writes, 'Each Beatitude inspires and challenges us at once.' That's true and it's also true of Dodson's book. Each chapter is both compelling and exposing."

John Starke, lead pastor of Apostles Church Uptown, New York City, and author of *The Possibility of Prayer*

OUR GOOD CRISIS

OVERCOMING

MORAL CHAOS

with the BEATITUDES

JONATHAN K. DODSON

An imprint of InterVarsity Press
Downers Grove, Illinois

InterVarsity Press
P.O. Box 1400, Downers Grove, IL 60515-1426
ivpress.com
email@ivpress.com

InterVarsity Press® is the book-publishing division of InterVarsity Christian Fellowship/USA®, a movement of
students and faculty active on campus at hundreds of universities, colleges, and schools of nursing in the United
States of America, and a member movement of the International Fellowship of Evangelical Students.
For information about local and regional activities, visit intervarsity.org.

Scripture quotations, unless otherwise noted, are from The Holy Bible, English Standard Version,
copyright © 2001 by Crossway Bibles, a division of Good News Publishers. Used by permission.
All rights reserved.

While any stories in this book are true, some names and identifying information may have been
changed to protect the privacy of individuals.

Published in association with the literary agent Don Gates of The Gates Group,
www.the-gates-group.com.

Cover design and image composite: David Fassett
Interior design: Jeanna Wiggins

ISBN 978-0-8308-4600-9 (print)
ISBN 978-0-8308-4826-3 (digital)

Printed in the United States of America ♾

InterVarsity Press is committed to ecological stewardship and to the conservation of natural resources
in all our operations. This book was printed using sustainably sourced paper.

Library of Congress Cataloging-in-Publication Data
A catalog record for this book is available from the Library of Congress.

P 25 24 23 22 21 20 19 18 17 16 15 14 13 12 11 10 9 8 7 6 5 4 3 2 1
Y 39 38 37 36 35 34 33 32 31 30 29 28 27 26 25 24 23 22 21 20

To the Lord of the Beatitudes

CONTENTS

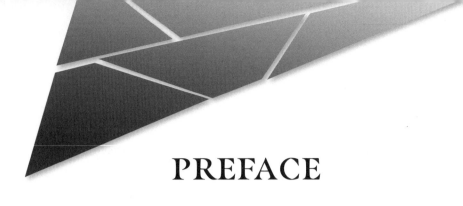

PREFACE

D O YOU EVER FIND YOURSELF in a state of existential vertigo? A flurry of issues swarm about us at any moment. How should I vote on gay marriage? Should I use traditional gender categories? What is my role in responding to the #MeToo movement? Should I advocate for security measures at the border? Is my smartphone really changing me? Should we pull down Confederate statues? What is a cultural Marxist? Why is it okay for Adam Levine to rip his shirt off at the Super Bowl and not Janet Jackson?

Many of these issues (and more) are not subjects for mere pundit debate. They touch down in the lives of everyday people. Like the conflicted parents who ask, "Should we attend our daughter's gay wedding?" Or the thoughtful friend who inquires, "Should I refer to my friend as 'They'?" Or the church member who asks, "How should I respond to that church member's post?"

Questions like these, and our society's polarized response to them, sent me back to school. The apologetics training I received in seminary is inadequate, given the real questions people want answers for today. This is no fault of my seminary; rather, it is a stark reflection of a change in the times.

And yet, there are many things that remain the same. The Word of the Lord is the same forever. Blessed are the meek, the mourners, the righteous, the merciful, the pure, the peacemakers, and the persecuted. These clarifying statements from Jesus possess such moral force they can flatten us like a Tyson Fury KO. But, when absorbed, they produce moral ballast that transforms our character, encourages our communities, renews our churches, and blesses our society. While we are in a cultural crisis, we're also in a moment ripe with tremendous opportunity. We can turn the tide, in small and big ways, by demonstrating *the goodness* of Jesus' kingdom.

Just a few minutes spent reflecting on the promises that come attached to the Beatitudes can lift us up like the whirlwind of God's love in a revival tent meeting: inherit the earth, yours is the kingdom, you will be satisfied, you shall receive mercy, and *you shall see God*. Jesus himself wants these promises, and his moral goodness, to break in now—in our lives, churches, communities, and countries.

While this book is the fruit of my study and reflection on some of these issues, it is not a work of academic apologetics or biblical scholarship, though I hope it stands up to scrutiny. Nor is it a comprehensive guide in how to counsel those who face these issues, although I hope it is a comfort and a guide. It is something in between, an attempt to imagine the goodness of the Beatitudes breaking into the crisis of our everyday lives. I believe the Beatitudes have the power and wisdom to center us in these dizzying times and bring the change we need.

One

FLOURISHING IN AN AGE OF CRISIS

A FTER SETTLING INTO MY TECH-SAVVY dining booth at JFK international airport, I heard "breaking news" in stereo. News blaring–flat screens scattered throughout the terminal announced CNN had obtained a tape of a conversation between Donald Trump and his attorney Michael Cohen discussing how they planned to buy the rights to a Playboy model's story of an alleged affair.

I looked around the terminal, scanning gates and bars filled with TVs. No one paid attention. Not a single person seemed to be concerned that evidence had surfaced indicting an American president of an extramarital affair, with a Playmate, which he tried to cover up by paying her off. Irrespective of political affiliations, this news should grab our attention. Not a head turned.

Why? Perhaps it's because we've become so accustomed to public crises. Just this week I came across the vicious ethnic cleansing of Myanmar's Rohingya, the massacre of six American women and three children in Mexico, an impudent religious leader hurling racial insults, impeachment hearings in DC, and a college admission scandal. If I'm honest, I'm kind of overloaded, even numb to these atrocities.

Every time we pick up our phones, we're hit with another calamity or scandal. And just when we think we can't process any more, a personal crisis hits.

I picked up the phone and said hello.

"Jonathan, this is Amy."[1] I hadn't spoken to my old girlfriend since she'd moved to Alaska a decade ago.

"Oh, hey, it's great to hear from you. How are you doing?"

"Well, okay. I've been meaning to call you for a long time. I need to tell you something. When we were dating, I got pregnant and had an abortion. I'm sorry I didn't tell you about it. I just felt like it would send you on a different path, away from ministry, so I kept it to myself."

Dead silence.

How do you absorb something like that on the phone? It took me a while to process what her words meant: my sin had led to the end of a precious human life. It had also placed my girlfriend in an awful situation. Clearly it had taken a lot of courage on her part to make this call. Eventually I replied, "I'm so sorry. I wish I had known so we could have made the decision together."

How would moral fortitude have changed that situation?

More self-control on my part would have made her life radically different. I regret my youthful lust, lack of self-control, and that I wasn't part of the decision she made. I contributed to a situation that led to an abortion. I hate that she had to suffer such a painful decision, alone. She was torn between two acts of compassion—compassion for someone she knew and someone she did not yet know. In what must have been a heart-wrenching decision, she chose me.

If I had been more responsible, Amy wouldn't have had to endure such a tormenting decision and undergo what some women describe as a humiliating procedure. If I had been morally upright, she also wouldn't have dealt with the guilt and shame that followed. I have wept at the thought of this, more than once. I have prayed, and pray even now, she experiences the comfort and forgiveness that only "the Father of mercies and God of all comfort" can provide, who comforts us in *all* our afflictions (2 Corinthians 1:3-4).[2]

Although it is understandable she didn't consult me, more honesty on her part would have radically changed my life too. If I had been part of the decision on whether or not to keep the baby, I would have advocated we keep and raise that eternal soul to the best of our ability. We probably would have gotten married. We would have raised *that* child. It's very likely I wouldn't have my wonderful wife of twenty years and our three precious children. I might not even be writing this book.[3]

Moral decisions create fork-in-the-road moments in our lives every single day. Depending on the decision we make, our actions have a positive or negative effect on ourselves and others: whether or not we tell our boss the truth that we blew it, whether or not we envy someone else's success, whether we choose to be generous with those in need, whether we sleep with our girlfriend or boyfriend, or choose to have an abortion.

I write this book, not as a paragon of morality, or the fountain of ethical wisdom, but as a redeemed sinner who is learning to so cherish the Lord of the Beatitudes that moral change happens.

If you can identify with a moral failure like mine, this book is for you. If you are currently struggling to live a life that pleases God, this book is for you. And even if you believe you've had only a few moral missteps, this book is for you. This book is for all who have failed to live up to the Beatitudes but want more. It is for those who want to mature, but aren't sure what next step to take. It is for those who recognize the moral chaos around them and want to do something about it. It is for anyone concerned about our *good* crisis.

AN AGE OF CRISIS

A new crisis appears in our newsfeed just about every day: #MeToo, the Charleston shooting, California fires, a school shooting, a nuclear threat. Crises *ad nauseam*. At times these crises grab us by the collar. Riveted, we track their developments, weigh in on the debate, maybe fire off a social-media post. If we feel strongly about the crisis, we may sign a petition, attend a lecture, or even join a march.

Then another crisis hits.

Headlines change overnight. With our empathy divided, we try to stay informed by scanning feeds, watching clips, and reading articles. But tension mounts as we juggle work, relationships, responsibilities, and the latest headlines. Overwhelmed, we lash out, retreat, or slowly grow numb. With exposure to an unprecedented flow of news—global in scope, around-the-clock in length, and often tragic in nature—the sheer volume of crises can overwhelm us. How are we supposed to absorb, much less cope with, so many calamities?

What is a crisis?

A crisis is a time of intense difficulty or danger that often requires thoughtful yet swift decision-making. When my mother's heart rate spiked to more than 240 beats a minute, the doctors in the emergency room had to make a quick but informed decision to avert a catastrophe. They decided to stop her heart.

So they charged the paddles up and shouted, "Clear!" Bewildered, my father stood by and watched the light fade from his wife's eyes. Her heart had stopped. Then the doctor hit her with the paddles again, this time restarting her heart. It worked. Her heart rate leveled out. Crisis averted.

In medical emergencies, we drop everything to attend to the person in need. The screams of a child cut through whatever we're doing and send us in search of the crisis. When we hear the dreaded words "They're going into surgery," we jump into the car, leaving dinner on the table. Suddenly everything else can wait.

While perhaps not as visceral, a financial crisis also snatches our attention. When we hear about an impending round of layoffs, we start floating our résumés. If the economy takes a hit, we scramble to make financial adjustments so we feel more fiscally secure. Nuclear threat? Pins and needles.

But if a big red banner stretched across our screen announcing "Breaking News: Global Moral Crisis," we'd keep on scrolling. That headline wouldn't even register. We wouldn't drop everything to solve the problem. Yet a moral crisis is more threatening than any other crisis. Why?

Because behind many crises is a moral crisis.

Behind the #MeToo movement is an insatiable lust for sex and control. Behind the financial crisis is an inordinate greed for more. Nuclear threat?—an unrestrained thirst for power. Moral calamity lurks behind most of the crises that solicit our attention, activating our thumbs to drive an opinion into our smartphones. Moral or ethical failure is often behind the crises that put us up in arms or down in the dumps. A failure of morals, not nerve, lurks behind scandal and injustice.

Just think what a little more self-control, honesty, and humility could do for the headlines. And what it could do for us. How would your story be different if, at certain points in your life, you chose the moral path, the right thing to do? Moral chaos exists in all of us, irrespective of political party, religious association, age, sex, gender, and race.

We are the moral crisis.

While some crises are moral in nature, others are natural, like my mother's medical crisis. Although it was very important to me, most of the world had no knowledge of it. My personal crisis wasn't a global crisis, and yet it demanded my attention. It's tempting to treat every personal crisis as a global crisis. When browsing social-media feeds, you'd think individual crises *are* universal crises. But a Facebook proclamation of a bad hair day is decidedly not a crisis.

So, what actually qualifies as a crisis?

THE CURIOUS ORIGIN OF CRISIS

The word *krisis* was used by the Greeks to refer to "a legal process of judgment." Aristotle used it to refer to a legal procedure that secured civic order.[4] In his case, it was a judgment that helped keep the city just and safe. A few hundred years later, Jesus used the same word to describe a coming day of judgment: "on the day of judgment [*krisis*]" (Matthew 10:15). He also used it to pronounce a future judgment that will separate the wicked from the righteous (John 5:22). But this judicial meaning of the word stretches back even further, past the Greeks to the Hebrews.

God created the tree of the knowledge of good and evil and placed it in the Garden of Eden (Genesis 2). The tree served as a kind of organic courthouse, reminding its observers of right and wrong. Trees frequently serve a judicial purpose in other places in Scripture. Deborah, a Hebrew judge, sat under a tree to pass her judgments (Judges 4:4-5). Absalom, the son of David, was caught in a tree and judged for sedition against his father (2 Samuel 18:9). Christ was judged on a tree for the sins of the world (Galatians 3:13). In the Semitic world, a tree often signified judgment. Similarly, when Adam and Eve ate of the tree of the knowledge of good and evil, God judged them and banished them from the Garden. But if they had abstained from it, humanity would have enjoyed the blessing of God's presence and provision forever. The original moral judgment was a *crisis* planted firmly in the ground.

Aristotle, Jesus, and authors of the Old Testament all used *krisis* to convey judgment.[5] The apple has fallen far from the tree. In their fascinating study on the etymology of *crisis*, historians Reinhart Koselleck and Michaela Richter describe how the word evolved from its original meaning of "a judgment regarding right and wrong" to "a change in the course of things." This change, they explain, is typically economic, medical, or historical in nature.[6] Over the centuries, *crisis* has been used to refer to matters that reach a boiling point, such as the coup of Napoleon III, German bankruptcies, English stock decline, and the American subprime housing crisis. This "boiling point" change in circumstances is often what comes to mind today when we hear the word *crisis*.

In the late twentieth century, *crisis* began to appear in news headlines frequently—in two hundred different contexts in 1980 alone. In 2019, we face an opioid crisis, a refugee crisis, a border crisis—and from a glance at my social media feed, a midlife crisis, a gaming crisis, a Captain Marvel crisis, and a bad hair day crisis.

Once a dense word referring to fixed moral judgments and powerful changes, *crisis* has devolved into a word that signifies momentary uncertainty. Will my hair turn out? Was Captain Marvel a good or bad movie? What will life be like after forty? We've relativized the meaning of *crisis* to such a degree that acceptable usage includes a tweet that reads "I'm in a parking spot crisis!"

How can this etymology of *crisis* help us better understand and address our chaotic times? Koselleck and Richter conclude, "The concept of crisis, which once had the power to pose unavoidable, harsh and non-negotiable alternatives, has been transformed to fit the uncertainties of whatever might be favored at a given moment."[7] The movement away from the original judicial sense of deciding between right and wrong—toward an individualistic, relativized meaning of *crisis*—reflects a broader philosophical shift. Subjective feeling is now more important than objective fact. A person's difficulty in finding a parking spot is a crisis, and it's more important than anything else going on at that moment. Individual perspective is what matters most.

The judicial meaning of *crisis* isn't the only thing that has changed. So has the judge. The locus of justice has shifted from the norm of "a tree" or courtroom to the whim of the individual. Individual comments on social media are frequently featured on cable news. Should personal opinion be given the same amount of weight as a subject-matter expert? Is there no moral standard to judge our opinions?

In this moral confusion, we're often tossed about in a sea of subjectivity, unable to address sudden changes in circumstances and society. Should I embrace transgenderism or insist on traditional gender categories? What should I do about the immigration crisis? Should I respond to that tweet or say nothing? We have lost the original idea of *krisis*.

Well, technically, *krisis* hasn't been lost; it has been replaced. We've replaced the tree of the knowledge of good and evil with a forest of individual opinion. One person cries, "Face the facts!" while another retorts, "Fake news!"

We need an arbiter of truth, a standard of justice to determine what is right and wrong. In the words of American diplomat and politician Daniel Patrick Moynihan, "Everyone is entitled to his own opinions, but not to his own facts."[8] If we're unable or unwilling to discern a norm to judge what is good and evil, the whole moral order will tumble into confusion. If we don't get the moral facts straight, a variety of "crises" will compound, and we'll sail into a very dark night.

We are in an age that desperately needs to know how to determine good from evil.[9] Without this moral discernment, we're unable to move toward human flourishing. How can this crisis be resolved? We must retrieve the ancient meaning of *crisis*—to go back to the Garden of Eden, so to speak, to rediscover what is good. This is urgent, not only because of the moral calamity "out there," but also because of the crisis "in here," in our hearts. Moral calamity respects no power. No person is off-limits. Just turn your finger around—look inward—and you'll find the crisis inside you. Lust, greed, power? Check, check, check. The seed of every crisis exists in every one of us. No one is immune. But if we can get a handle on our moral turbulence, we can contribute not only to our own good but also to the good around us.

WHAT IS GOOD?

Despite the moral fissure in our society, we still recognize and admire virtues in those around us. In 2018, the world watched as Thai divers attempted a complicated rescue of a boys' soccer team. Trapped in a cave, with the only exit submerged in water, the boys needed expert help. The Seals risked their lives as they swam through the narrow passage to reach the boys. When the divers arrived, they gave them food and training in how to use scuba gear. Then, in an hours-long trip for each boy, two divers accompanied them out of the cave. Sgt. Saman Kunan, a former Thai navy Seal and triathlete, died when he ran out of air during his return from delivering oxygen tanks to the boys. He was hailed a hero.

All the rescuers displayed character traits like *humility*— thinking of others as more important than themselves. They also displayed *mercy*, giving up their own oxygen—and in one case, life itself—to enable the boys' survival. The divers received awards and were widely praised for their good character.

What makes their actions good? Where does our notion of good come from? Historically Western society has functioned with a sense of goodness grounded in Greco-Roman philosophy. Aristotle described virtue as the "mean" between two extremes. Courage is the mean between being cowardly and being foolish. Generosity is the mean between stinginess and lavishness. We pick up on this moral distinction when, wanting to promote generosity, we say, "Don't be so stingy! It's not like you have to empty your bank account." We appeal to the mean. However, aiming for the mean isn't enough. For the Greeks, virtue ethics located "the good" not merely in moral action but also in the moral agent himself. What we do *is the fruit of who we are.* True goodness requires integrity.

When goodness becomes who we are, not just what we occasionally do, we become virtuous. When I was a kid, I ate sticks of rock candy that had the word *Brighton* stamped on the end. No matter how much I licked, the word didn't disappear. The letters seeped all the way through.[10] Virtue is like that. No matter how far down you go, goodness still shows up.

As a young parent, I often got upset when one of our kids spilled something or refused to obey, but as I matured, the virtue of patience began to ripen in me. Now my reaction to a spill is to assure them they have done nothing wrong and to help them clean it up. Patience has become my kneejerk reaction, at least with spilled milk. Unfortunately it's not always present when they disobey. Patience hasn't seeped all the way through me yet.

Moral integrity requires significant seeping—that is, an alignment between our public and our private lives. What we do in the dark should stand up to the light. Failures in this alignment hit the headlines regularly. The "best-known, and perhaps best-liked" of the people exposed in the year of #MeToo was news anchor Matt Lauer, who confessed to "inappropriate sexual behavior."[11] Aren't success and a great family enough? Not if *power* goes to the head. Beloved actors and musicians, such as Wesley Snipes and Willie Nelson, were prosecuted for tax evasion. Are the millions of dollars not enough? Not when *greed* gets into the heart.

But before lining up celebrities to judge, we should pause to consider what journalists would turn up in *our* lives if they went digging. The public/private division of ethics isn't restricted to public figures. We, too, harbor greed. One research group reported that evangelicals give about 4 percent of their income to churches, and Christians in general give only 2.43 percent—far less than the 10-percent tithe.[12]

In the wake of #MeToo, a string of high-profile ministry leaders were exposed for sexual misconduct, prompting yet another hashtag: #ChurchToo. This revealed a tendency among Christians to overlook sexual abuse within their own communities, often dismissing concerned parties as "overreacting." The painful truth is that this kind of assault often begins when victims are young. Although Rachael Denhollander is known for her high-profile, eloquent witness against US Olympic gymnastics doctor, Larry Nassar, for his serial sexual abuse of gymnasts, this was not Denhollander's first experience with sexual abuse. That occurred when she was seven, at the hands of a trusted Christian and family friend.[13]

Whatever happened to being salt and light in a bland, dark world? Perhaps Christians have settled for *appearing* good without *being* good. Sure, we *do* some good things. But unless we're *intending* to do them, those actions are not virtuous; they're just good luck, says Aristotle. Virtue is intentional, not accidental. Integrity works to hold our public and private life together. Character is stamped all the way through.

What matters most to you: how you are seen in public or what you actually do in private? Do you want people to *think* you're a good person without doing the hard work of *being* a good person? When we become more concerned with keeping up appearances in public than cultivating virtue in private, we contribute to the crisis around us. We're sitting ducks for the next scandal. No one is a passive observer in this crisis; all are participants.

What role will you play? Will you settle for a veneer of goodness or dig deep to forge character that bleeds through?

THE GREATEST MORAL DOCUMENT

If we want to make progress in virtue and to contribute to the greater good, we need training for goodness. Jesus is an excellent person to look to. His morality was contained not only in what he taught but also in how he lived. He incarnated the virtues. Jesus was *humbly* submissive to his heavenly Father and to Roman authorities in the most difficult of circumstances. Instead of swimming in the current of pharisaical first-century self-righteousness, he showed radical mercy toward social and religious outcasts. He risked *everything* for them.

Jesus was also righteous beyond any moral indictment, to the point of receiving the approbation of the Roman governor, Pontus Pilate, during his trial. Jesus persevered, not only through ridicule and abandonment, but also through unjust, harrowing torture. On top of that, he forgave his enemies while naked and hanging by iron spikes, which they drove into his hands and feet. Jesus is an example of virtue ethics par excellence. He embodied what he taught. There was no fissure between the public Jesus and the private Jesus; he was righteous all the way through. How can we embody the character of Christ and embed his virtue in our souls?

Jesus' most famous sermon is the Sermon on the Mount. Among other things, it lays out a guide to the virtuous life. In the first twelve verses alone, the sermon calls for humility, mercy, purity, righteousness, peacemaking, *and* endurance (Matthew 5:1-12). Even atheists admire Jesus' teaching. Evolutionary biologist and impassioned atheist Richard Dawkins wrote, "Jesus was surely one of the great ethical innovators of history. The Sermon on the Mount is way ahead of its time."[14]

To solve the crisis of good, we need something ahead of our time. We need an objectively true guide that originates beyond us to redefine us. Historian Jaroslav Pelikan points us in the right direction when he writes, "The Sermon on the Mount remains the greatest moral document of all time."[15] If this sermon is true and its author lived the teachings to a tee, then surely this is the place to start.

The Sermon on the Mount gets its name from where it was delivered. And it was probably delivered more than once—on a mount and on a plain (see Matthew 5–8; Luke 6:17-49). The location of its delivery also tells us something about the constitution of the preacher. Jesus delivered this sermon from an elevated and exposed place, enabling him to broadcast his message to many people but also allowing him to receive objections from his detractors. He challenged prevailing notions of the good without protecting himself.

Of course, just reading the greatest moral document or embracing moral philosophy is not enough to cultivate goodness. Like the Greeks, Jesus shared the conviction that goodness requires symmetry. His sermon calls for alignment between inner desire and outward action. Emphasizing purity, he said, "Blessed are the pure in heart, for they shall see God" (Matthew 5:8). But purity of heart is not enough; the heart must overflow. Jesus also said, "Out of the abundance of the heart, the mouth speaks" (12:34), making a heart-and-speech connection. Purity of heart leads to purity of action. The Beatitudes challenge both the inner and the outer person, both act and being, making them an excellent guide to character formation.

While there is no doubt Jesus' sermon resonated culturally with Greco-Roman virtue ethics, his message was also informed by his Jewish tradition. As we will see, he repeatedly drew on words, concepts, and passages from the Old Testament to present the good life. In his book, New Testament professor Jonathan Pennington states the main thrust of the Sermon on the Mount: "[It] is offering Jesus' answer to the great question of human flourishing, the topic at the core of both the Jewish wisdom literature and that of the Greco-Roman virtue perspective, while presenting Jesus as the true Philosopher-King."[16] Indeed Jesus presented a convincing message on human flourishing not only as a sublime moral philosopher but also as the King of the world.

THE BEATITUDES

The sermon opens with a series of declarations—beatitudes— that call for goodness. *Beatitude* is a strange but compelling word. It comes from the Latin word *beatitudo*, which is a translation of the Greek word *makarios*, meaning blessed, favored, or flourishing. The Beatitudes show us eight ways to live a blessed life (or nine, depending how you read Matthew 5:10-12).

What exactly is the blessing in these one-liners? One way to read them is as if-then promises of the future. If you keep the *if*, then in the future you will get the blessing. If you are "poor in spirit," then you will get the blessing of "the kingdom of heaven." If this is the correct way to read the Beatitudes, it means we can secure future blessing in heaven by living a moral life now. The challenge, of course, is in determining whether or not we have been "poor in spirit" or "pure in heart" enough?

Another way to read the Beatitudes is as a promise of future blessings *for the present*. Live poor in spirit now, and you'll benefit immediately—get a foot in the kingdom, so to speak. Hunger and thirst for righteousness now, and you will get a taste of eternal satisfaction. This certainly fits with the "future logic" of the New Testament, in which there are frequent exhortations to do something in the present based on future realities: "For this perishable body must put on the imperishable. . . . Therefore, my beloved brothers, be steadfast, immovable, always abounding in the work of the Lord" (1 Corinthians 15:53, 58).[17] Paul argues that the promise of the resurrection of the body should improve the quality of one's work now. Or consider, "You may not grieve as others do who have no hope. For since we believe that Jesus died and rose again . . . God will bring with him those who have fallen asleep" (1 Thessalonians 4:13-14). The promise of Christ's return provides hope in present grief. When we trust in these "heavenly" truths, they stamp goodness into our souls. Some suggest that the best way to read the Beatitudes is with both of these approaches in view.[18] I agree.

Jesus' sermon casts a vision for how we're meant to flourish in this world. Pull on the heavenly promises, and you find character is attached in the present. The Sermon on the Mount provides a guide to the good life in both its everyday ethics and its eschatological promises. Like a pitchfork, it goads us to good action, but it also dangles a carrot: heavenly promises for present times. The sermon addresses habit by luring us with a glorious vision of existence: "Blessed are the poor in spirit, for theirs is the kingdom of heaven. . . . The meek . . . shall inherit the earth. . . . Those who hunger and thirst for righteousness . . . shall be satisfied" (Matthew 5:3, 5-6). In other words, be poor in spirit because you are a citizen of the kingdom of heaven. Be meek because you are someone who, only in Christ, deserves to inherit the world. Be righteous because you're so satisfied in God you need not stoop for anything less. In this way, the Beatitudes present a guide and a pledge for human flourishing.

Wouldn't it be nice to live on an earth filled with humble, virtuous people? Just think of the impact on traffic, conflict, and the headlines! Who doesn't want to live satisfied *forever*? In the Beatitudes, Jesus promises the world we all want, where the just, the true, and the good saturate everyone and everything. He offers a vision of true and total human flourishing. So each time you read the word *blessed* at the beginning of a Beatitude, think of the glorious possibilities of living the way Christ taught.

SECULAR BEATITUDES

Of course, the good life doesn't come without hard work. The requirements are steep: a modest life, a humble heart, and righteous character—not exactly a piece of cake. Although the sermon inspires with a glorious vision of reality, it also intimidates with real-life expectations. Quite honestly, the Beatitudes can seem otherworldly—not merely because of where they originate, but also because of how we operate down here on earth. I mean, how would the Beatitudes read if we rewrote them to reflect the way we *really* live? What would a brutally honest list of "secularized" beatitudes look like?

If you could cut one or two Beatitudes, which would you drop from the list? Perhaps the ones about the righteous or the perse-cuted or those who mourn? What might you add? "Blessed are the driven, for theirs is the kingdom"? "Blessed are those who are true to themselves, for they will be happy"? I like "blessed are the comfortable, for they will never have to sacrifice." And to borrow a line from rapper Kendrick Lamar, "Blessed are the liars, / For the truth can be awkward."[19]

Before we can leap into the Beatitudes' promise, we have to evaluate our functional beatitudes—how we really think and live. To do this, let's consider each beatitude in its secular context—a way of living that functionally removes belief in God from everyday actions and replaces it with ingrained cultural patterns of thinking and behaving.[20] For instance, in the secular context, *mourning* is an unwelcome but unavoidable part of life. How do we handle that sadness? When faced with disap-pointment, heartache, or suffering, we often opt for escape—take a trip, go to a movie, train for a marathon, or binge Netflix. But when we choose to escape, we don't cease to believe. We simply believe as though God has nothing to offer us, and in his place, our chosen escape does. *We mourn in an age of distraction.*

This secularizing impulse removes God from his place of power and substitutes the self. When the self is center stage—even if it's poor old me—*meekness* becomes just about impos-sible. It's hard to be humble when no one stands taller in our thoughts than ourselves. In the Age of the Big Me, righteousness is an off-putting word because it suggests narrow, dogmatic thinking.[21] We prefer to sort things out for ourselves, to be open-minded. As a result, our functional belief is that we're satisfied, not by being righteous, but by being ourselves.

We tend to prefer tolerance over mercy and self-expression over purity. In theory, we all like the peacemakers, except when we're called on to make the peace. Most of us would rather avoid conflict or escalate it.

Then there's persecution. Not a lot of volunteers for this one! But Jesus said, "Blessed are those who are persecuted for righteousness' sake, for theirs is the kingdom of heaven" (Matthew 5:10). How do we embrace persecution when what we love is ease?

Virtue is an uphill battle in the age of the big comfortable Me. It's easy to see how individualistic, self-centered, secular beatitudes could lead to a moral unraveling, a crisis of the good. If everyone is out for themselves, who helps the marginalized? If we're true only to our desires, how do we build and maintain a just society? Jesus guarantees the kingdom of heaven: the just, true, good world we all want, where beauty saturates everyone and everything. Of course, it won't fully arrive until the King returns, but it can begin with being poor in spirit.

Is it possible to avert a moral crisis in a secular age? Can we reap the benefit of Jesus' stirring promises now? I believe so. If not, Jesus is a fraud. This single sermon, admired by secular humanists and Christians alike, is central to averting catastrophic and moral failure. It's also the key to human flourishing. So let's get to work in making good out of our crisis.

Two

POOR IN SPIRIT
IN AN AGE
OF THE BIG ME

"Blessed are the poor in spirit,
for theirs is the kingdom of heaven."

MATTHEW 5:3

I WAS RAISED IN AN EAST TEXAS TOWN nestled in
the piney woods, "the oldest town in Texas." It's divided by
a railroad: north of the tracks, people more affluent; south of the
tracks, less affluent. For a few years, I lived on the south side of
the tracks, in a rental house with my parents and two brothers.
My father worked hard as a window cleaner to provide for the
family, and my mother cultivated a home warmed by her hospitality and love. On Sundays, friends often came over after
church to enjoy a home-cooked meal and lounge around in
fellowship as we waited for the groaning of the homemade ice-
cream machine to stop. In many respects, I was rich with blessing.

However, every once in a while we'd come up short in paying the bills. We'd pray, ask God to provide, and wait. Then my parents would check the mailbox or bump into a friend at church and receive an envelope with "just enough" in it. These surprises enabled us to pay for school expenses or get the car fixed. People of greater means helped us when we were "poor." I'm grateful they did.

My childhood experience of lower-class living is nothing compared to how many people in the world live. In Central America, half the population lives below the poverty line. My first trip there was a mission trip to Merida, located on the Yucatan peninsula, home to the stairstep Mayan pyramid called Chichen Itza. Each morning we gathered to pray at the local church, an open-air structure with a cement slab, four wooden poles in each corner, and a makeshift covering for a roof.

After prayer we went door to door to tell people about Jesus. Stepping over trash and waste, we walked to homes made of corrugated cardboard, tarpaper, and cinder blocks. I was invited into one home that was so dark, it took minutes for my eyes to adjust. Eventually I realized there were several people in the single-room home. About halfway up the wall, a whittled tree hung horizontally as a shelf, with a few dishes delicately balanced on it. A flickering candle provided light. There was no running water. As we shared the gospel with them, I couldn't shake the jarring images of poverty. I wondered, *Are these the people Jesus was referring to when he said, "Blessed are the poor in spirit, for theirs is the kingdom of heaven"? Do they have an advantage in the kingdom of God because of their poverty? Has upward mobility driven me further from the kingdom?*

POOR IN SPIRIT

In the Gospel of Luke, Jesus states this Beatitude differently: "Blessed are you who are poor, for yours is the kingdom of God" (Luke 6:20). He addresses the poor themselves, not the poor in spirit. Some see this as warrant for a special focus on the economically poor, interpreting it *literally* as "God favors the poor." This interpretation led to what's been called "the preferential treatment of the poor."[1] Does this mean people of character make concern for the economically impoverished a priority? If so, how should people who are *not* poor respond?

Jesus was once approached by a wealthy man who asked him how he could enter the kingdom of God. Jesus told him to sell all his possessions and give them to the poor. Is this what Jesus requires? *It may be.* He may be calling you to leave the comfort of your life and enter the discomfort of service to impoverished people, and perhaps even to sell all your belongings and move to a Majority World country in need of economic development.

But before you pack, consider that economic development and poverty relief require resources—wealth. Moreover Jesus and Paul invited those who were of a high socioeconomic status into the kingdom of God without requiring them to take a vow of poverty (Luke 7:1-5; Acts 17:4, 12). So while Jesus did emphasize ministry to the poor—and he challenges our attachment to wealth—he doesn't require everyone to take a vow of poverty. In fact, he had disciples from higher classes who supported his life and ministry, including Joseph of Arimathea, "a rich man" who paid for Jesus' burial (Matthew 27:57-59), and women of means who supported Jesus' ministry (Luke 8:1-3).

So "poor in spirit" must mean something other than self-imposed poverty.

The religious me. This Beatitude is also interpreted attitudinally, meaning Jesus intended for us to take on an attitude of poverty. This would mean taking an impoverished view of yourself. Instead of focusing on the poverty of others, think more poorly of yourself. Don't think, I have so much to contribute. Look at me. Rather acknowledge you have nothing to contribute to God. Confess that you're spiritually poor: "I'm destitute before you."

The word *broken* is sometimes used to describe this attitude. Perhaps you've heard this advice: "You need to be spiritually broken to be used by God." In my early twenties I followed this path, along with other college students seeking to honor God. I found myself repeatedly praying, "Lord, break me. Show me my weakness. Show me my sin." I fasted and prayed frequently. I believed self-imposed humility was the way to please God; only then would I break through the wall of my sinfulness and be truly good. As I reflected on that season of my life, it became clear I was misdirected. I had been unaware of a subtle spiritual pride that permeated my prayers—an assumption that if I could constantly see myself as little, I would arrive.

The problem with this approach was that I remained big.

My spirituality was about me, not about God. I became obsessed with my moral and spiritual performance, often agonizing over my failure. This led to cries to be humbled even more. Even if you can't relate to this, many of us obsess over our inner state in one way or another.

The therapeutic me. In his landmark article "The 'Me' Decade and the Third Great Awakening," literary journalist Tom Wolfe critiqued various movements of the sixties, a time he dubbed the Me Decade. He noted the narcissistic trend of focusing on "me" as people began to think more and more of "human potential." Psychotherapy catapulted into popularity, with Carl Rogers's "client-centered" therapy dominating US self-help books, classes, and workshops. Therapy sessions multiplied like rabbits, and the human potential movement was off to the races.

Wolfe described these movements as a kind of me-centered religion: "They begin with the most delicious look inward; with considerable narcissism, in short. When the believers bind together into religions, it is always with a sense of splitting off from the rest of society. We, the enlightened (lit by the sparks at the apexes of our souls), hereby separate ourselves from the lost souls around us."[2] Sound familiar?

Cloaked in noble goals, these movements were often more about self-discovery and self-distinction than humble service to society or to God. Today the self-help industry is still thriving, with prominent authors often outselling blockbuster novelists. Personality tests are especially in vogue. Why? Often because they are about *me.* We love getting into ourselves and understanding ourselves, even if the discovery is disappointing. In the words of Wolfe, these movements have a "beat that goes . . . Me . . . Me. . . . Me . . . Me . . ."[3]

When trying to understand what it means to be poor in spirit, we must be careful not to focus on attaining it ourselves. As the late Dallas Willard noted, Jesus did not say, "Blessed are the poor in spirit *because* they are poor in spirit."[4]

The selfless me. What then does "poor in spirit" mean? A literal reading concludes that flourishing comes to the poor and to those who grant them preferential treatment in some way. A spiritual reading construes blessing as reserved for those who see themselves as small, not big.

What if we took the best of both views? New Testament scholar Scot McKnight takes this approach: "The socioeconomic rootedness of the word 'poor' does not permit exclusively the spiritual poverty interpretation, and the 'in spirit' demands that this be more than simple economic oppression."[5] However, he limits his application to *the poor*, maintaining the poor in spirit are "the economically destitute who nonetheless trust God."[6] McKnight unites economic poverty with spiritual faith. Although this combination is attractive, it still restricts the Beatitude to the socioeconomically poor. While the poor are certainly in view, this Beatitude has a lot to say to all of us.

To be poor in spirit is to be genuinely humble *and* in touch with those humbled by circumstance (whether you are poor or you care for the poor). British minister and doctor Martyn Lloyd-Jones described being poor in spirit as having "a complete absence of pride, a complete absence of self-assurance and self-reliance."[7] The poor in spirit do not isolate themselves from those in need, nor do they elevate themselves as needy or broken. They are, in a sense, selfless. They renounce the status obtained through success, and they serve those who lack what they have. They give from what they have: finances, wisdom, affection, encouragement, and service. They are generous because, as Jesus said, "theirs is the kingdom of heaven."

HUMBLE AND GENEROUS

Tom and Julie Steller live in an old three-story house on Elliot Avenue in Minneapolis. When my wife and I lived with them, they had five children ranging in age from one to fifteen. That alone would keep most of us busy, but the Stellers have an indomitable capacity to give. They lived on the second and third story, while we lived on the first. Two single men lived in the basement. We were all charged next to nothing for rent, while the Stellers lived on a modest income. When anyone needed a ride, they were the first to offer their beat-up conversion van. When someone needed a place to stay, they were always willing to open their doors. But they shared more than just square footage; they shared their lives.

It was our first year of marriage, and my Texas belle, Robie, found herself in a new community with a new last name, living in a land unfamiliar to her—the North. We endured the second-harshest winter in recorded Minnesota history to date. On difficult days, when Robie's earrings froze to her ears in subzero temperatures, Julie lent her a listening ear, a sympathetic heart, and wise counsel. They often met in the stairway that connected the upper and lower levels of the house. Julie chose to put Robie first, despite the fact there were a thousand other things she could be doing.

The Stellers would pray for us at the drop of a hat. One evening, as I was leaving to go to a speaking engagement, I met Tom coming up the sidewalk. He paused to ask about me. Sensing my nervousness, he smiled, gently laid his hand on my shoulder, and prayed for me.

As it turns out, scores of people have reaped similar deposits of generosity. Neighbors freely pop by, and kids gather to shoot basketball in their driveway. When a dispute arose in the neighborhood, neighbors turned to Tom. People felt they could approach the Stellers and ask for help or counsel, because they were humble people. They never held anything over anyone, and they certainly didn't boast in their generosity.

Tom went on to found a graduate school for theology students, and Julie a handcraft goods company that employed stay-at-home moms and the down-and-out. But they would never introduce themselves as the founders of anything. Why? Because they are humble and generous.

I thank God for the Stellers' example of what it means to be poor in spirit, and especially for Julie's friendship and wise counsel, which helped us survive the winter of our first year of marriage. In his book *The Road to Character*, David Brooks describes people of strong character as humble, not thinking of themselves at all—*and* as people who get things done.[8] He could have put "the Stellers" in parenthesis next to his description.

THE BIG ME

Practicing poverty of spirit can be difficult, and it certainly doesn't come overnight. None of us is the first or the last to be confronted by our own self-centeredness. However, each generation is intoxicated with the self in different ways. The Age of the Big Me stretches beyond Wolfe's Me Decade into the present Selfie Generation. If we are to address the good crisis by becoming more humble and generous, we must understand how the Big Me shapes us.

Outward activist to inner me. Although history doesn't follow neat demarcations, "the sixties" was a decade of considerable upheaval. It began with the bright vision of Kennedy's New Deal, and after his assassination, Johnson tried to reboot the country's optimism with the promise of the Great Society. However, both initiatives faded as the war on poverty was replaced by the war in Vietnam. Millions of Vietnamese and 58,000 US servicemen died in the controversial conflict. The struggle for civil rights erupted over gross racial segregation and discrimination against African Americans. Newspaper headlines announced demonstrations regularly; bombings occurred at home and abroad; and strident conflict charged the atmosphere. As the country reeled from political and social turmoil, it was undeniably divided.

That decade wasn't the only one to experience division. The seventies weren't much better: Watergate, a massacre at the Munich Olympics, the kidnapping and Stockholm syndrome of Patty Hearst, and the serial murders of Ted Bundy. Clearly our times aren't the only times of crisis. This might be good to remember next time we're tempted to throw up our hands in despair.

As anxiety and frustration mounted in the sixties, many people turned to protest, including Jerry Rubin.[9] With a mop of brown hair and a distinctively thick beard, Rubin was a flamboyant anticapitalist protester. He helped mobilize national protests against the Vietnam War and the 1968 Democratic

National Convention, resulting in a very public, even comedic, trial. He arrived at the trial wearing a judge's robe covering a Chicago police uniform. Later he campaigned to elect a pig as the president of the United States and dropped dollar bills onto the floor of the New York Stock Exchange. In many ways, he outdid the social activists of today. But in the seventies, his radical ways came to a screeching halt. The next time he surfaced, he was on Wall Street, working as a successful entrepreneur, enjoying what money could buy.

Why the sudden about-face? Rubin became so outwardly focused, he felt his activism had caused him to lose touch with who he was. As a result, he began a journey into himself. Over the span of five years, he immersed himself in therapy. He tried EST, meditation, modern dance, humanism, and hypnotism; began to eat healthily; and got a haircut, shaved, and lost thirty pounds. He emerged proclaiming he had learned "to love myself so that I do not need another person to make me happy."[10] Like many of his contemporaries, Rubin sought salvation through a journey into the self. Retreating from the chaos of the sixties, he began to live for himself, not for causes or society, the future or the past.

The activist me. Interestingly the two poles of Rubin's life reflect two contemporary difficulties in becoming poor in spirit. On one extreme, we're consumed with causes and activism. As in the sixties, there are many issues to confront: racism, gender inequality, sexual assault, gun control, immigrant crisis, climate change, adoption, and abortion, to name a few. However, if others don't take up our cause or retweet our concern, we find it tempting to look down on them. If they disagree with us, we may lash out in anger. Social media exacerbates this tendency, where our anger devolves into rants, threads, blocks, deletes, and ghosts. Civility is increasingly rare.

The meekness associated with being poor in spirit is hard to cultivate. We feel the pressure to pick a cause, stand out in the crowd, get things done, and identify with a movement. But if we embrace a cause-driven life, our worth will become inevitably tied to our activism. Our identity can become so fused to a particular issue, we lose touch with what it means to flourish. Anger, bitterness, distrust, and division creep in. Humility and generosity of spirit leach out. It becomes almost impossible to value those who aren't a part of our cause. Like Rubin, we lose touch with what it means to be human.

The inner me. The other difficulty we face is a preoccupation, not with causes, but with the self. Who am I? What's my passion? What do I identify with? These questions mirror, to some extent, Rubin's shift from outward activism to inner exploration. Our preoccupation with the self today tends to emphasize self-expression over therapy. Reflecting on this broad cultural shift, historian Christopher Lasch wrote, "People today hunger not for personal salvation, let alone for the restoration of an earlier golden age, but for the feeling, the momentary illusion, of personal well-being, health, and psychic security."[11] This pursuit of the self is expressed through constantly changing fitness programs, fad diets, and self-help apps. Writing in the late seventies, Lasch noted a "collective narcissism" in which people become connoisseurs of their own decadence, cultivating a "transcendental self-attention."[12] That's an apt term for an age consumed with the digital self.

Transcendental self-attention seems to have become more public than therapeutic. It's widely accepted to focus on self by honing an individual brand narrated on Twitter or Facebook, displayed on Instagram, and viewed on YouTube. We're encouraged to have avatars, identities, handles, and icons that represent our unique selves. Entranced by our screens, we open, scroll, and swipe, eager to discover what others have to say about us. If we encounter disappointment, we may post just to get a reaction or check again a few minutes later for a friendly dopamine boost. In the absence of a cause, we fixate on the self.

Many selves. However, we no longer curate a single self. Our pursuit of self-distinction is no longer restricted to a single vocation or role. In premodern times, an individual was a farmer, a milkman, a homemaker, or a blacksmith. But now we conceive of ourselves as many things. Postmodern philosophers, such as Derrida and Foucault, came along and said there is no self, no truth, no grand explanatory narrative to navigate life. In this vacuum of identity, meaning, and story, people began to look for identity in many selves, patching together meaning from various, often competing stories. Since the single self failed to hold weight, we turned our attention to various modes of self-expression. We combine any number of identities for worth: the successful professional, the doting mother, the hip single, the thoughtful reader, the indie music expert, the caring husband, the social activist, the justice crusader, the über-blogger, the pietistic Christian, the fashion expert, the startup genius, and so on. There is no essential me; I can become whatever I construct myself to be.

As our many selves proliferate, it becomes difficult to keep up with reality. In fact, some of us redefine reality. Rachel Dolezal reconstructed her race, insisting she was black when she is, in fact, white; Bruce Jenner reconceived his gender, insisting his soul was female, even though his anatomy was male; and Brian Williams misconstrued his actual experience, writing himself into stories that he was not a part of. With a divided self, life becomes a carnival, and the self becomes an assortment of masks.[13]

Social media bios often boast this range of identities. We project whomever we want to be, and we have platforms to broadcast our selves. If we get bored or down, we garner a temporary lift—or a permanent dollar (the Kardashian cash-in)—by "posting" to our identity of the moment.

Capitalism rewards those who post most often and most uniquely.

We're exploited with indie and artisan everything. Indie music, organic food, vegan subculture, hipster fashion, essential oils, niche shopping for phone covers no one else has. When one identity fades, there's always another one waiting. All the while, we are losing our true selves.

The band Broken Bells articulates our identity crisis:

The open doors left me wanting more . . .
It's another way to win a useless fight
You've been lying so long don't know you're faking.[14]

The self-deceit underneath our selves can become so powerful that we no longer recognize the lie we've spun. Contending for worth through many selves is a useless fight.

The cost of following the self. This fixation on the self is also dangerous.[15] It makes deep, lasting friendships and marriage difficult to achieve. About half of Americans report chronic loneliness. The inundation of many selves is psychologically destabilizing, and even the success of a single identity doesn't promise satisfaction, as high-profile suicides demonstrate. In fact, suicide rates have risen sharply, increasing 24 percent between 1999 and 2016.[16] That's thirteen suicides per one hundred thousand people, the highest rate recorded in twenty-eight years. Suicide is now the tenth leading cause of death.[17] Although there are various factors in any given suicide, and mental health is a serious concern, researchers found that more than half of people who died by suicide didn't have a diagnosed mental health condition at the time of death. Although it's impossible to know for sure, the spike in suicide rates may have something to do with our untenable many-selved quest for meaning and identity.

Whether we embrace a cause, dive deep into the inner me, or take varied trips into many selves, the Big Me is not working. Self-exploration and self-expression are not sufficient sources for personal worth. The Big Me turns out to be a shriveled me. The relentless search to find ourselves within the frame of personal experience is endless. We need something to break through the frame of our self-aggrandizing experience. We need transcendent hope.

But in order to receive such a hope, to embrace the possibility of redemption, we must face down our self-centered sins. We must confess that our causes, techniques, journeys, and selves are not enough. We must come to the point where we realize that our greatest offense is not failing to love ourselves but failing to love and enjoy God. For only a transcendent God with an infinite capacity to love can satisfy our desires. But first we must look in the mirror and name the Big Me and its self-righteous activism, obsession with self, or self-focused masquerades—or any combination of the three.

BOWING DOWN FOR HOPE

So how do we escape the Big Me and find lasting worth? By being poor in spirit. In Hebrew, the word *poor ones* (*anavim*) means "bowed down." Why are the poor bowed down? In some cases circumstances have forced them down, but when Jesus adds the phrase "in spirit," he prevents a circumstantial reading. Being poor in spirit has to do with our posture, not just in front of circumstances or ourselves but before the face of God.

It has everything to do with *where we look*. Some of us look inward—in comparison to self. Others of us look outward—in comparison to others. But those who look up—in comparison to God—start to see. When we look at ourselves in the light of God's outstretched greatness, we are not above average; we are deficient. Looking up, we realize our abject poverty before God; we have not a cent to contribute to the Creator, who fashioned everyone and everything. Every single breath is a debt to his towering, creative greatness. This is the crux of being poor in spirit, as Martyn Lloyd-Jones put it: "It is nothing, then, that we can produce; it is nothing that we can do in ourselves. It is just this tremendous awareness of our utter nothingness as we come face-to-face with God."[18] That truth is hard to embrace, perhaps most of all, because poor in spirit requires nothing of us.

The most important person. I had the crazy idea that going on a five-hour field trip to NASA with fifty fifth-graders would be a good idea. As a chaperone to three kids, I was tasked with not letting them out of my sight. On the way to NASA, one of them told me about a summer camp he went to. He said, "I didn't really like it because they made us sing to God every night and listen to someone talk about him. I mean, I believe in God, but I just think you should keep him on the side."

I thought about what he said and replied, "If God is the most important person in the world, don't you think he should be more than 'on the side'?" He stared at me blankly for a moment, then looked away and said, "I guess." When we sideline God, something has to take his place. Up sprouts the Big Me.

There's only one person worth adoring forever: the most important person. If that person is you or me, we're doomed. Seriously. But if that person is outside our frame and off the charts in humility and grace, that would change things. Jesus Christ is that person. "Have this mind among yourselves, which is yours in Christ Jesus, who, though he was in the form of God, did not count equality with God a thing to be grasped, but emptied himself, by taking the form of a servant, being born in the likeness of men. And being found in human form, he humbled himself by becoming obedient to the point of death, even death on a cross" (Philippians 2:5-8). Jesus emptied himself so he could fill us with his undying love. He humbled himself to the death so he could give us life. Jesus bowed down so that he could lift us up. It wasn't any ordinary person who did this for us; it was the most important person: "Therefore God has highly exalted him and bestowed on him the name that is above every name, so that at the name of Jesus every knee should bow, in heaven and on earth and under the earth, and every tongue confess that Jesus Christ is Lord, to the glory of God the Father" (Philippians 2:9-11). Every knee will bow, by force or by faith. Jesus is that great. Those who bow the knee now get to enjoy eternal life. Those who do not will face an eternal death. Jesus uses his authority over everyone and everything to allow his creatures to tear his flesh to pieces and nail him to a cross. Why? So the wages of sin would be paid, so the debt would be cleared, and so knowing and enjoying his eternal love could begin. Now.

Jesus says that eternal life is knowing the only true God and his Son Jesus Christ (John 17:3). That's heaven breaking into earth, a down payment on the promise of future inheritance, present riches for the poor in spirit. Confessing our sins before the face of this God, and enjoying his radiant love and for-giveness, is a blessing. And it's a blessing that continues: the poorer we get, the richer we become. The more we stare into the endless glory of God, in the face of Christ, the more we enjoy his grace. With these riches in hand, we are compelled to live as Jesus did—humbly and generously—so others can get in on the early inheritance.

THE KINGDOM OF HEAVEN

How then do we cultivate poverty of spirit? By living out our citizenship in the kingdom of heaven. The kingdom of heaven gives us many insights into how to develop character. I'll mention two.

Follow others' examples. First, consider the architecture of the kingdom of heaven. We often think of heaven as a disembodied existence in the clouds or an individual paradise, but the kingdom of heaven is neither. Jesus' kingdom is a kingdom of people. It teems with life, with people from every culture interacting, learning, and creating, all before the face of God. So the kingdom of heaven is a communal kingdom.

In Isaiah 61, when God proclaims good news to the poor, they become content, liberated, and joyful. The poor in spirit are many, not one. In fact, the subject of all the Beatitudes is plural not singular—the poor, those who mourn, the humble, the merciful. Every subject is plural, which means Jesus isn't calling just individuals to the character of the kingdom; he's calling a whole community—the church—to be poor in spirit. This is the first insight of the kingdom. We need one another to become what God has called us to be. And this is by design not flaw. We are meant to change, to become poor in spirit, with the help of others.

One way to do this is by absorbing the examples of others. Remember the Stellers? They showed me how to be poor in spirit. But they didn't just show me; they rubbed off on me.

Get around people who are poor in spirit. Have them over for dinner, go out for coffee, ask them to mentor you. Heck, move in with them! Invite some friends to challenge you in your pursuit of humility and generosity. Ask them to check in on you to find out who or what you are bowing down to. Look for a church, or if you're already in one, commit to it. Become a member of the community; join a community group. Invest in others, and ask them to invest in you. We're changed when we look out for things we admire in others and then, instead of pushing them away because of those admirable things, imitate that part of them. It's very hard to absorb the good in others when we're living an individualistic life, when we're not an active part of the kingdom of heaven.

Formed by God's Word. It isn't as though, upon reaching heaven, we summit our comprehension of God and cease to obey him. In biblical descriptions of heaven, we find something very interesting: people continue to learn there (Micah 4:2). If you want to close the gap between where you are and where you want to be, you need not just any community but a learning community.

Now, most people use the term *learning community* to refer to a way to advance a career or hobby, but I'm talking about advancing our character and knowledge of God. Christians should be people who are always learning, but not in an abstract Bible study sense, though Scripture is integral. Anyone can accumulate biblical knowledge while acquiring more pride. The knowledge has to go somewhere; it can go to your ego or it can go to service. This is why Jesus said,

> Therefore whoever relaxes one of the least of these commandments and teaches others to do the same will be called least in the kingdom of heaven, but whoever does them and teaches them will be called great in the kingdom of heaven. For I tell you, unless your righteousness exceeds that of the scribes and Pharisees, you will never enter the kingdom of heaven. (Matthew 5:19-21)

The kingdom community isn't just teaching; it's doing. In it we learn to *obey*. Jesus commissioned his disciples to make other disciples by "teaching them to observe all that I have commanded you" (Matthew 28:20). Paul said of immature Christians that they are "always learning and never able to arrive at a knowledge of the truth" (2 Timothy 3:7). Why don't they arrive? Because they don't obey. They don't put learning into service of others.

Are you in a kingdom community? Are you opening the Scriptures and applying them with others week to week? If not, don't expect to become poor in spirit. It's impossible to be humble and generous when we aren't looking at something greater and more gracious than ourselves. Humility and generosity need a target; we need others to serve and a great God to worship.

The kingdom of heaven is breaking into this world through God's people. If you are already a citizen by the grace of God, live like it! Don't settle for the kingdom of self. If you are not, then take a knee and call out to this unmatched Savior. Join a community in which you are accountable to people who challenge you, who are hard to love, and who don't click with you—people who challenge your preferences and expose your sins. This will send you back to the face of God, where you'll rediscover his humble love and profound forgiveness—all at Jesus' expense. You'll find the King of the kingdom, the only one worth bowing down to.

OVERCOMING YOUR CHAOS

Virtue isn't accidental; it's intentional. In *Hamlet*, Shakespeare wrote, "Assume a virtue, if you have it not. . . . For use almost can change the stamp of nature."[19] We must form habits in order to overcome the moral chaos in and around us. Here and at the end of each chapter, you'll find questions like the following to help you cultivate a Beatitude in your life.

- Do you favor preferential treatment of the poor or embracing an attitude of spiritual poverty? What action can you take to grow where you are weak in this?

- Tell God how you feel about becoming poor in spirit. What beliefs drive those feelings? Ask God to address your beliefs and feelings to produce true humility of spirit in you.

- Do you tend toward inner me or outward activist? How is that identity inadequate?

- Identify a community in which you can invest more time. Who in that community is poor in spirit (humble and generous)? What can you learn from them?

- To become truly poor in spirit we have to look at something greater than ourselves. Read Psalm 8 and jot down some great things you see about God. Pause to admire them and to praise God for them.

Three

MOURNING IN AN AGE OF DISTRACTION

"Blessed are those who mourn,
for they shall be comforted."

MATTHEW 5:4

WITH TEARS STREAMING DOWN HER FACE, she described the horror of the school being lit up with gunfire. As she ran, bodies fell behind her—thud, thud, thud. The terrifying sound—rat-a-tat, rat-a-tat—filled the air. People hid, crouched, screamed, and cried. Then a final shot silenced the horror. Mourning erupted.

We absorb this all-too-common scene through screens. We watch the investigation unfold. Names of the deceased are released, and flags are lowered to half-mast. The country tries to assemble sense out of mayhem. Debates over gun control flare up, rants flood into social-media channels, and many grow numb unwillingly. Then a notification pops up on the screen, and we switch gears.

Mourning is now stimulated by copious information streams.

A constant flow of tragic knowledge overwhelms us, triggering everything from outrage to resignation. In 2018, almost 70 percent of Americans reported feeling "news fatigue."[1] We simply aren't made to handle the scope and depth of suffering in the world, so we turned off our TVs. But the news kept coming via Facebook, Twitter, and Instagram, outlets through which we can instantly express our sorrow.

The age of distraction is changing how we grieve. Yet Jesus' timeless Beatitude promises comfort: "Blessed are those who mourn, for they shall be comforted" (Matthew 5:4). How do we mourn in an age of distraction?

DEALING WITH SORROW

How do *you* mourn? Think of a personal sorrow: getting laid off, being betrayed by a friend, experiencing marital conflict, suffering with gnawing loneliness, losing a loved one, or receiving a bad medical report. How did you respond? What did you do with your emotions? Where or to whom did you turn?

When disappointment strikes, many of us try to *minimize* our sorrow: "It's not that bad." "It's really not that big a deal." "I'm just waiting on Mr. Right." Friends chime in with platitudes: "There's a better job waiting for you." "Just think, it could have been worse." They minimize sorrow too.

But what about when the pain resurfaces? When it just won't go away? Pick up the phone? Eat some ice cream? Surf the net?

During heavy seasons of counseling, when I'm overwhelmed by the suffering and pain in those I counsel, I'm tempted to distract myself from sorrow. I come home from work, greet the kids, and try to enjoy dinner with the family. When the kids are in bed, I unconsciously drift toward the pantry or fridge—not just once, but two or three times. I find myself standing there, silver doors propped open, face aglow, scanning for sweets. Harmless, right? Not if I keep sidelining sorrow. My waistline expands, and patience with the kids shrinks. I find myself easily frustrated by small challenges and disappointments. I snap at others. These are signs I've been ignoring my sorrow.

What are your signs? Some of us throw ourselves into work, arriving early or staying late at the office. As we invent deadlines, perfect processes, and fine-tune reports, work becomes a convenient way to avoid pain. When you're caught off-guard by the memory of a disappointment or loss, you just tell yourself, "I'll process over the weekend or when I'm on vacation." But then, during a late night at the office, you begin roaming the internet. You end up clicking on ads your well-rested self wouldn't fall for, then tumble into an unexpected shopping spree. Or an unexpected image appears on the screen. You click, and before you know it, you're burying your sorrows in a digital fantasy. You go home guilt-ridden, your sorrow pushed even further down.

Others *maximize* their sorrow by obsessing over a lost job, friend, or dream. Mourning begins to color everything. What started out as understandable discouragement ends up changing your outlook on everything. It's like someone throws a hood over your head. Thoughts become dark and isolating. Everything seems to be headed down, not up. Though friends try to cheer you up, gloom becomes a companion. Enthusiasm for things you used to love drains away. Despairing thoughts and depression creep in. Alternatively you might exploit your disappointment through shouting, crying, or fits of rage. The anger filters through you as snap judgments, snide remarks, and a cynical view of everything, especially "the media."

Why do we minimize and maximize our sorrow? On the surface, it seems to be a very unhealthy thing to do. We dismiss or expand our sorrows because, deep down, we're unsure what to do with them. While expressing our emotions is certainly a way we deal with disappointment, it's not enough. Emotions alone do not have the ability to resolve things. An important question lurks behind our emotions: Why? Why did this happen? In the words of Nietzsche, "A man can endure almost any how if only he has a *why*."[2]

MEANING FOR MOURNING

Victor Frankl was an Austrian neurologist arrested by Nazi authorities and sent to Auschwitz. There he was forced to dig a tunnel for a water main, day after day, unaided and often without eating. While trying to scratch out a living in this death camp, he watched many suffer brutally and die. Some took their own lives.

Frankl took many fellow prisoners on as patients. In his best-selling book, *Man's Search for Meaning*, he recalls watching a patient who, upon his last breath, was immediately ransacked by other prisoners for shoes, clothes, and string. Rail-thin prisoners laboriously dragged the dead body up two six-inch steps, the head bouncing. Then they cast the body onto a pile of other corpses. As he sat down to eat his soup, Frankl looked up to see the dead patient's eyeballs staring at him. Unmoved, he could think only about survival.[3]

How did Frankl survive? Why did he not take his own life? During his imprisonment, he frequently recalled Fyodor Dostoyevsky's words "There is only one thing that I dread; not to be worthy of my sufferings." Frankl embraced this challenge and came to the conclusion that suffering is a *moral task*. This aspiration—a belief that it is good to endeavor to live worthy of our sufferings—kept him alive. You could say he found a *why*.

Most of us will never suffer like Frankl, but he offers us an answer to lurking questions. "In some ways suffering ceases to be suffering at the moment it finds a meaning, such as the meaning of a sacrifice."[4] He came to the conclusion that suffering is a moral task that requires *meaning*. He appealed to meaning to coax fellow prisoners out of suicide, imploring them to consider what the future held for them. One laborer expressed a longing to be reunited with a child in a distant country (love). Another aspired to finish a series of scientific books (vocation). By embracing meaning, each one learned to persevere under the harshest of circumstances. And it worked! They survived.

Do you have a meaning strong enough to help you embrace the task of suffering? Or does suffering consistently take you by surprise? Frankl's patient-prisoners answered the question "why do we mourn?" with a meaning deep enough to cope with Auschwitz. While it's humbling to place our own sufferings next to those at Auschwitz, we can honor their suffering by allowing them to inspire us to suffer well. To do this, we must consider why it's hard to suffer well.

CONTEMPLATION IN A DIGITAL AGE

One challenge is what British psychologist Guy Claxton calls our "inner psychology of speed."[5] Our modern, technological age has created a way of thinking driven by efficiency and pace. Our wheels are always turning at a rapid rate. If we cease to produce for too long, we become restless. Contemplating meaning is hard when spare moments are filled with phone in hand.

Contemplation requires quiet, stillness, and focus, practices rapidly disappearing in our society. At Duke University, full-length books are infrequently assigned to undergraduate students because they are unable to finish reading them.[6] Studies show that while students can write internally coherent paragraphs, they often can't track a sustained line of an argument. They're losing their ability to focus.

But students aren't the only people struggling with this. In his best-selling book *The Shallows: What the Internet Is Doing to Our Brains*, Nicholas Carr explains how our brains are being rewired by use of the internet and social media. He concluded, "The Net may well be the single most powerful mind-altering technology that has come into general use."[7] Mind-altering? Surely this is an exaggeration?!

Decades before Carr, communications theorist Marshall McLuhan wrote *Understanding Media* in which he boldly claimed, "The medium is the message."[8] This claim is powerfully relevant today. The message that affects us most may not be the content of our technology but the technology of the content. The form of delivery is just as powerful as the content delivered. It's not so much the tweet but the fact that we read and move past it so quickly. It's not just that there was a school shooting but that we absorbed the school shooting without reflection, fired off a social-media response, and then moved on. The medium—in this case social media or twenty-four-hour news—shapes us more than the news itself. We grow numb to tragedy, dismissive of profound aphorisms, and inclined to outrage. This distorts our sense of what's urgent and even beautiful.

Have you ever come across something utterly fascinating in the moment that, looking back, wasn't that impressive? One morning as I was on my way into a staff meeting, I checked Twitter and saw a video of a man boxing a kangaroo. I was so mesmerized, I interrupted the meeting—twice—to show everyone.

Now, I'm all for a good laugh, but was that video important enough to interrupt a staff meeting? Was it really that urgent? Aren't the salvation of souls, care for sufferers, and the truths of Scripture more urgent, important, and beautiful than a boxing kangaroo? Yes, the medium is the message. Consider how often this kind of thing happens in any given week. The same week, I heard about a tragedy in a foreign country and told myself, "I just don't have the bandwidth to process this right now." But I did have the capacity to process the boxing kangaroo.

The medium as the message is also operative when reading online. As we skim an internet article, we may glance at a GIF in the sidebar, quickly read a pop-up ad, toggle over to respond to an email, toggle back to the article, skim some more, respond to a notification, and forget to finish the article—all while listening to Leon Bridges. We're crazy if we think this isn't affecting us. Neuroscientists point out that this rapid, fragmented consumption of information rearranges the neurons in our brains. As a result, the ability to keep a train of thought or to kick back and meditate becomes increasingly undesirable, and even difficult. Our reading habits rewire us for rapid consumption of data, not reflection. Is it any wonder that even a little suffering can throw us off? We lack the reflective habits necessary to discover and relish meaning that makes hardship a moral endeavor. Instead we view suffering as an inconvenience or inefficiency.

Of course, reading habits can be changed easily by using various apps or programs to prevent notifications from popping up and to shut programs down. We can disengage from the net. We can pick up a trusty hard copy, which has no wires at all. But when we do slow down enough to contemplate our sorrows, we don't always like what we find. Theologian Paul Tillich explained that people who endure suffering are taken beneath the routine busyness of life to find out they aren't who they believed themselves to be. Reflection can be arresting. We don't always like what we see![9]

Have you ever been shocked by your thoughts in a season of difficulty? Something at work isn't going well. You get into your car and pull onto the highway. Someone cuts you off. You lay on the horn and then think about catching up with them to shoot them the bird or bump their vehicle from behind. Hypothetically speaking, of course! Perhaps in the heat of conflict and hurt you've uttered the words "Fine, let's get a divorce!" Or "I just don't want to live anymore." Suffering draws our darkness to the surface, and to deal with it, we need not just meaning but also comfort for our sorrow.

SOLACE IN SORROW

When we encounter something difficult and are willing to accept it, we often say something like "I'm okay with it" or "I have a peace about it." But is this *comfort*?

When Jesus promised comfort, he didn't appeal to a vague feeling of inner tranquility. Instead he promised an actual comforter. Among the various Greek words that can be translated *comfort*, Jesus selected the word *paraklētos* to refer to the Holy Spirit (John 14:16, 26; 15:26; 16:7).[10] In doing this, he referred to the Spirit as one who comes alongside. When hardship hits, we want someone to take notice and come alongside us. This longing is often behind our pain-tinged tweets, texts, and posts. We're reaching out for comfort, validation, understanding. So while Frankl is right to point us to *meaning* to get through suffering, perhaps more profound is the fact that he himself took the place of *comforter* to those around him. It wasn't merely his ability to coax articulated meaning out of his suicidal friends that enabled them to survive. *It was his presence.*

A friend had betrayed me. By gossiping behind my back, he sought to ingratiate the compassion of others and turn them against me. His primary accusation was that I was "unapproachable" as a leader and therefore unfit for leadership. I took this accusation seriously. As I considered it, I realized I had a habit of cutting people off in conversation. If I thought I knew where they were going with something, instead of allowing them to finish, I announced their conclusion and then affirmed or challenged it. I realized this was arrogant and inconsiderate, so I apologized to my team. Although I occasionally sense the temptation to cut people off, by God's grace I've learned to eliminate this habit almost entirely. I do want people to feel valued, not tolerated.

However, the charge that I was unfit for leadership remained. One by one, our leadership team fell under my friend's spell, until it looked as though I would have to resign. I was overcome with confusion, grief, and dismay. As I considered the Scriptures, prayed, and sought counsel from others, I could find nothing disqualifying me from serving as an elder.

Sitting on my couch, I received a text from another friend asking how I was doing. I replied, "Not well." He offered to drop by. When he arrived, he came into the living room, sat down next to me, and asked me a question. For some reason, his presence gave me permission to collapse. Between sobs, I blurted out an incomprehensible answer. He didn't ask for a clarification. Instead he put his arm around me and let me sit there and cry like a baby. He didn't try to fix me or give me counsel; he simply entered into my sorrow and prayed for me. I have no recollection of what he prayed, but his presence is burned into my memory. His *presence* was inexplicably comforting. He had come alongside me.

The presence of comfort. This is what Jesus promised to those who mourn: the presence of comfort. What he didn't promise is that friends will always be there to comfort us. At times they will be busy, disinterested, unavailable, or in sorrow themselves, unable to come alongside us. Not everyone can break away in the middle of the day and come sit on your couch.

This is where Jesus' promise of a comforter comes in. Although Jesus is no longer present to put his arm around us, he has sent his Spirit, the Comforter, to be with us: "But when the Father sends the Comforter [*paraklēte*] instead of me—and by the Comforter I mean the Holy Spirit—he will teach you much" (John 14:26 TLB). The Spirit is the *portable* presence of God. Those who trust in Jesus receive the presence of the Comforter. Wherever we go, he goes. Consider this poetic promise of the Spirit's presence:

> Where shall I go from your Spirit?
> Or where shall I flee from your presence?
> If I ascend to heaven, you are there!
> If I make my bed in Sheol, you are there!
> If I take the wings of the morning
> and dwell in the uttermost parts of the sea,
> even there your hand shall lead me,
> and your right hand shall hold me. (Psalm 139:7-10)

Even your best friend can't do this. The Spirit is a mobile comforter who awakens us to the mercies of God, custom-fit for every occasion. Writing to comfort a church in Corinth, Paul said, "Blessed be the God and Father of our Lord Jesus Christ, the Father of mercies and God of all comfort, who comforts us in all our affliction" (2 Corinthians 1:3-4). Both the Father and the Son possess mercy and *all* comfort to help the afflicted. In *all* our afflictions. Every single one counts.

The picture emerging from these texts is quite stunning: The Father, Son, and Holy Spirit act as a divine community of comfort for those who are in Christ Jesus. The Trinity possesses *all* comfort *all the time* for *all afflictions*. The Godhead never run short and are never indisposed. They are an eternal fountain of self-giving solace for sufferers. Always available, together they provide comfort that is both portable and eternal. Nothing can hold a candle to that.

After my friend got up from the couch, hugged me, and left, waves of sorrow continued to crash against me. I felt as though I were sinking. Arms outstretched, I cried out to God for mercy, asking him to save me. Everything I had built, everyone I'd trusted, seemed to be falling away, brick by brick, like the dismantling of a dream.

While I was in this state, my wife received a message from a friend who felt compelled to tell me that though I was sinking like Peter, who tried to walk on water to Jesus, Jesus would reach out to me and pull me up. How could she have known I was sinking? My wife hadn't told her. There I was, in the uttermost part of the sea, and a text message reached me, mystically attached to a Comforter who knew right where I was and drew me to his consoling presence.

Minutes later I received a phone call that turned the tide. This call led to a significant change in my team. Perspectives shifted, relationships were reconciled, and profound change occurred. I retained my role, and our church went on to thrive.

All of this mourning led me into deeper meaning and into the Presence. Suffering yielded intimacy with my Savior. I now know God to be an eternal, portable, loving Comforter at a deeper level than I ever knew before my trial. There are some things we can't learn without going through the storm.

MOURNING THE EVIL WITHIN

But what if our sorrow is the result of our own failure? How do we find comfort when we screw up? Jesus' promise of comfort comes from Isaiah 61, where both *comfort* and *mourn* are used in relation to Israel's sinful failure. As a result of their disobedience, Israel was exiled from God's presence. The nation was mourning what they had become: a rebellious, God-diminishing people.

Israel's mourning put them in touch with deeper meaning and longing. Isaiah said, "A Redeemer will come to Zion, / to those in Jacob who turn from transgression" (59:20). A transgression— that is, a misstep—sent Israel into exile. But it wasn't just one misstep; it was many.

The phone call I received from my ex-girlfriend telling me she'd had an abortion wasn't the result of a single misstep. It was one among many. Like Israel, I too had diminished the value of God, seeking satisfaction in sex instead of in him. Eventually the longing for reconciliation with God and a morally pure life became so intense that I renounced the evil of my God-spurning pursuits. A hunger for more took its place.

The root of Israel's suffering was also *personal evil*—trading the eternally good and present God for empty, vain idols. As Jeremiah the prophet said,

My people have committed two evils:
they have forsaken me,
the fountain of living waters,
  and *hewed out cisterns for themselves,*
broken cisterns that can hold no water. (Jeremiah 2:13,
  emphasis added)

To enjoy the comfort of living water, and to honor God, we must pry our hands off broken cisterns. Thirst cannot be quenched from porous vessels. We must turn from transgression to taste satisfaction.

Jesus promises comfort to those who mourn not only the evil committed *against* us but also the evil committed *by* us. He extends solace for the crisis within and the crisis without. Very often we're quick to condemn social evil but slow to recognize personal sin. Outrage flares up at those who do wrong outside us, but we have a much higher tolerance for the rebellion *inside* us. This softening of personal sin and heightening of social evil is inconsistent, not least because the seeds of moral crisis grow within each of us.

Comfort for moral failure comes only when we face up to our sins and mourn them, recognizing that we too have walked away from our great Friend and merciful God. If we experience no contrition for sin, then character change is unlikely. But blessed are those who mourn *their* sin, for they shall be comforted. Paul wrote it this way: "Godly grief produces a repentance that leads to salvation" (2 Corinthians 7:10). If we want to enjoy God's mercies, we have to look him in the face and admit our transgressions. We must learn to practice godly sorrow.

There is a time to weep. We can choose it or it will be chosen for us. When is the last time you wept over your sin, when you mourned the evil not just out there but also in yourself? King David said of his unrepented sin,

> When I kept silent, my bones wasted away
>   through my groaning all day long.

For day and night your hand was heavy upon me;
> my strength was dried up as by the heat of summer.
> (Psalm 32:3-4)

The heavy hand of the Lord will eventually come upon us if we tolerate inner evil. Our joys will lose their luster. We will become emotionally frail, easily snapping at those around us or falling into despair. But mourning points to real meaning: real inner evil and real forgiveness.

In Isaiah, God promises to pour out an oil of gladness in place of mourning, to comfort those who mourn. David sang,

> I acknowledged my sin to you,
> > and I did not cover my iniquity;
> I said, "I will confess my transgressions to the LORD,"
> > and you forgave the iniquity of my sin. (Psalm 32:5)

When we are honest with God about our sins, forgiveness and comfort come rushing in. When we get beneath the routine busyness of life and discover we aren't as noble or moral as we thought, mourning in the presence of the Comforter guides us to a better version of ourselves. We find our identity as we are forgiven, loved, and acquitted—in Christ, where gladness, strength, and comfort abound. This process of confession, repentance, and faith in Christ leads to a moral reordering of our lives. As a result of our encounter with the mercies of God, we're moved to live in a way that draws us closer to the fountain of his comfort. We are wooed to goodness, which in turn sends goodness back into our relationships, communities, and world. So learning to mourn meaningfully actually helps address the crisis of good around us.

HEAVEN WORKS BACKWARD

But what is the blessing that Jesus promises to those who mourn? He said, "Blessed are those who mourn, for they shall be comforted" (Matthew 5:4). Certainly this blessing comes through the comfort God offers in our sins and sorrows, but he also promises a future comfort. Some sorrows are so deeply painful, so horrifically awful, it is hard to associate blessing with them. We are tempted to conclude, as one character in C. S. Lewis's novel *The Great Divorce* blurted out to an angel, "No future bliss can make up for it."[11]

The Comforter allows space for such laments. After all, Christ himself declared to God, "Why have you forsaken me?" (Matthew 27:46). This same Jesus promises that those who mourn in hope will not be disappointed; they will be comforted.

The comfort we gain in the present state of things is a comfort that will one day grow, enlarging to encompass the whole world. The hands of God will wipe every tear and refashion the world into a place of never-ending comfort and joy. It isn't so much that the presence of this future bliss will "make up for" our agony, but that it will radically reframe it. In response the angel says, "Heaven, once attained, will work backward and turn even that agony into a glory."[12]

How will heaven turn our agony into glory? The new creation will put all sorrows in their place, not by diminishing evil but by revealing that it is harnessed for good. After enduring betrayal, isolation, human trafficking, imprisonment, and slander, Joseph concluded that what others intended for evil, God intended for good (Genesis 50:20). Joseph didn't diminish his sufferings as less than evil. Quite the opposite; he assigns them to their mastermind, Satan. Yet, at the same time, he looked back on his agony with his eyes on glory. How? He both trusted and saw *the good*. He obtained future comfort in the present.

Joseph trusted in a God who superintends evil for good. His God was not asleep while he was sold into slavery, something he no doubt struggled with at the time. Yet he was able to look back and see some of the good God had worked through a complex set of providences—good he could never have conceived at the bottom of his pit. Through the evil of trafficking, Joseph was put in place to strengthen the economy of a superpower that provided food for surrounding nations during a great famine. Through his imprisonment, the eternal soul of a baker was saved. Through isolation, God met Joseph in dreams and visions. And through Joseph's rise to power, the nascent nation of Israel was preserved, from which the Messiah of the world would come.

In a sense, Joseph gives us the vantage point of heaven. He shows us that God superintends evil for good, making an agony a glory. He was able to see that his suffering purposefully fit into a complex, providential plan for good for countless others. He is proof that heaven works backward.

But Joseph's life offers us more than proof; it offers us a way to trust when we don't see the proof of our agony becoming glory. We can know future comfort now by trusting the Person who chose not to remain in heaven to orchestrate good but descended to earth and suffered to secure that good. Those who trust in this God *will be comforted*, both now and forever.

Sorrows are part of the call to follow Jesus. And only in falling in behind our great Captain, digging in and standing in the trenches of suffering, do we get to fight for the ultimate cause, which is an eternal meaning and presence we easily lose sight of: the hope of the glory of God. As the apostle Peter wrote,

> Beloved, do not be surprised at the fiery trial when it comes upon you to test you, as though something strange were happening to you. But rejoice insofar as you share Christ's sufferings, that you may also rejoice and be glad when his glory is revealed. If you are insulted for the name of Christ, you are blessed, because the Spirit of glory and of God rests upon you. (1 Peter 4:12-14)

The Spirit of glory guides us into that greater glory. He is present to remind us of God's promises and to imprint them on our soul, where we experience undeniable comfort and joy from his companionship. And one day we will, upon seeing the face of Christ, order every suffering under his, recognizing that our sorrows are worthy of the suffering Savior who makes all things new.

So don't settle for meaningless mourning. Insist on more. Slow down to contemplate the promises and presence of God. Try to avoid minimizing or exaggerating sorrows; take them to the Comforter. Put all things in perspective by trusting in God's promise to superintend evil for good and in Jesus' promise to bless those who weep, knowing heaven can and will work backward.

OVERCOMING YOUR CHAOS

- ◆ What are some specific ways you maximize or minimize your sorrows? Write them down. Confess them to God and share them with a friend.

- Think of a meaning that can better help you embrace suffering as a moral task. Read Romans 8:18-39. List the "meanings" God provides as ways for us to navigate our sorrows. How can you remember them?

- Think of someone who is suffering. How can you practice a "ministry of presence" toward that person?

- Read Psalm 139. Write down all the ways God is a comfort. Encourage someone with what you discover.

Four

MEEKNESS
IN AN AGE
OF HUBRIS

*"Blessed are the meek, for
they shall inherit the earth."*

MATTHEW 5:5

W E RARELY THINK OF OURSELVES AS PROUD.
Instead we think of others—"the arrogant guy," "the
stuck-up girl"—who seem to excel in pride as if they work at it.
People from the entertainment industry may come to mind:
Rosie O'Donnell, Christian Bale, or Beyoncé. Or from sports:
Floyd Mayweather, Draymond Green, Nick Kyrgios. Pride is
easy to spot in those who are in the limelight but difficult to see
in ourselves. When a video of Bale losing his temper and cussing
out a camera crew went viral, people spewed judgments at him
online. We often judge a high-profile person for an instance of
arrogance, one explosion of anger, or a tirade rife with

profanities, as if we've never done the same thing. We reduce people to the madness of a single moment.

STRONG PRIDE

In 1976 a survey asked people to list their life goals. Fame ranked fifteenth out of sixteen goals. A recent survey reported that now 51 percent of millennials say being famous is "one of their top personal goals."[1] Why is fame attractive? To be famous is to get the attention of others through a personal quality or skill. That alone is benign. But when our *ambition* is to attract attention, we dip into pride.

I want to be known as a good author. Part of that is noble, as I want my writing to be reliable, insightful, and helpful to others. Above all, I want to glorify God, not myself. But when another author in my field attracts attention, pride sometimes comes knocking. If my first impulse is to celebrate her success, I know humility is operative. But if I think, *What? I've written better on that topic! Why didn't my book get that much recognition?* I know I've crossed over into the land of look-at-me.[2] Pride seeks the applause, the glory.

C. S. Lewis clarified the nature of pride when he wrote,

We say that people are proud of being rich, or clever, or good-looking, but they are not. They are proud of being richer, or cleverer, or better looking than others. If everyone else became equally rich, or clever, or good-looking there would be nothing to be proud about. It is the comparison that makes you proud: the pleasure of being above the rest.[3]

Pride rears its ugly head when I compare myself to someone who appears to be more successful. I want to look as good as, if not better than, that person. Strong pride lurks in many of us. It's that impulse to seek attention from others, even applause: What did they think of my outfit? Did I impress them with my presentation? Did anyone comment on my post?

WEAK PRIDE

Not everyone struggles with strong pride. Weak pride fixates on self in a self-deprecating way rather than an attention-getting way. It's found in the person who says, "I'll never measure up. I'll never make it. I shouldn't even try. I should just quit." There are a lot of I's in those statements, a symptom of weak pride. Instead of pandering for applause, anemic pride wants to be accepted. It's in the person with a poor self-image prone to self-loathing. Instead of looking down on others, she looks up, because weak pride wants approval. While some measure of approval is healthy, a persistent craving for it springs from unhealthy comparison. It's the result of comparing oneself to others *negatively*: "I'm not that attractive, athletic, successful, smart, creative, moral." "I wish I was like so and so." Strong pride gloats in ability, but weak pride wallows in inability.

Those of us who struggle with weak pride are often silent. We may serve others without complaint, but we track every self-sacrificing act. Or we get engrossed in the past, focusing on how we've been mistreated and deserve better, or on how we don't measure up. We're keenly aware that we fall short.

In Ernest Hemingway's short story "In Another Country," a soldier is injured and sent to a military hospital. There he meets other soldiers who have been injured in combat and awarded various medals. When they ask why he got his medal, they discover his injury was an accident, not the result of valor. As a result, he's treated differently. After cocktails at night, he finds himself "imagining himself having done all the things they had done to get their medals."[4]

Do you ever imagine yourself doing things others have done? Have you fantasized about being selected for that promotion, giving that advice, or speaking at that conference? Is it wrong to aspire to these things? Aren't they good things? Yes, but they're not *our* things. When we imagine ourselves in someone else's place, we steal what belongs to them. We cross the line of valor into vanity, moving from humility to pride.

MIDDLE PRIDE

Both weak and strong pride are forms of self-centeredness. They emanate from preoccupation with ourselves, with how we're viewed and how we compare. However, there's a kind of middle pride somewhere between the two. It says, "Define *yourself.* Stand up for *your* truth. Be *yourself.*" It is weak because it's consumed with how we feel: oppressed, misunderstood, slighted. It's strong because it attempts to self-correct by fixating on an attribute, preference, or opinion. It gloats in self-expression.

Some fundamentalists display middle pride when furiously picketing gay pride marches. Standing on the sidewalk with signs that read, "God hates fags," they invoke the Almighty to champion their view. They're standing up for "their truth," but it rubs us wrong. Why? Because it's fueled by pride and hate.

They aren't alone in this. Progressives do similar things. In the 2018 Women's March in Dublin, Ireland, angry protestors held up signs reading, "May the fetus you love be gay. Keep your rosaries off our ovaries." They too were standing up for "their truth," but they were oppressing others with it. Those with middle pride glory in the ideals of the self, expecting others to honor them no matter what. Middle pride is intolerant of those who disagree with or challenge the self.

The very notion of "my truth" can be a type of hubris, because it puts self at center stage. It insists individual opinions or preferences are central in the metaphysical universe. To claim a personal opinion as truth is to take possession of the truth. When we do this, we co-opt the classic definition of *veritas*, which belongs to no one. For instance, the truth of gravity does not belong to a single person or group. It is universally true that things that go up must come down. Regarding nonscientific matters, we should surely debate what is true by giving our reasons, but we need not supplant the truth with the self. This is a momentous move of hubris—replacing the ideal of truth with the preference of self.

British philosopher and essayist G. K. Chesterton wrote, "What we suffer from today is humility in the wrong place. Modesty has moved from the organ of ambition. Modesty has settled upon the organ of conviction, where it was never meant to be. A man was meant to be doubtful about himself, but undoubting about the truth."[5]

Now we're doubting about "the truth" and undoubting about "my truth." This is a power play, something American-Russian journalist Masha Gessen noted of Vladimir Putin, who "asserts power over the truth."[6] If we are to cultivate true humility, we need to relocate meekness to the organ of the self and allow truth to stand in its transcendental, time-tested place.

However, there is a courageous version of standing up for "my truth." The #MeToo movement put the evils of sexual assault on display by empowering victims to tell their true stories of assault and abuse. The men and women who went public with their stories bravely owned what happened to them. This step can be very difficult for victims because of the feelings of shame and social stigma associated with abuse. But the act of telling others actually weakens the lie that the abuse was their fault. It allows the victim to actually embrace "their truth"—to tell the true story of their suffering and call for justice. In cases like this, a person actually lines their story up with *the truth* of what happened. They are not asserting power over the truth, but allowing the truth to challenge those in power. May their tribe increase.

TRUE HUMILITY

As it turns out, all three forms of pride are distorted views of the self. But humility gives us a true view of self. It isn't impressed by self-importance. It navigates between the rocks of strong and weak pride and forgets who is in the middle. Humble people aren't preoccupied with themselves. Martyn Lloyd-Jones commented, "We spend the whole of our whole lives watching ourselves. But when a man becomes meek he has finished with all that; he no longer worries about himself and what other people say. To be truly meek means we no longer protect ourselves, because we see there is nothing worth defending."[7] This self-forgetfulness is a tall order in an age of hubris, but when we see it in others, we are drawn to it.

Socially renewing humility. Will Campbell was an activist, a friend to Martin Luther King Jr., and a minister to the incarcerated. He was so widely respected, his obituary appeared on the front page of the *New York Times* in 2013. One day he took a team to minister to inmates at the Tennessee Department of Correction. As his team approached the entrance, a guard stopped them and said they couldn't enter, based on an apparently invented objection: a team member's shoes were inappropriate for a prison visit. When Will asked for leniency, the guard snapped, "One more word out of you, and none of you will see anyone here today!" Put off, they drove an hour round trip to a nearby town to purchase shoes. When they returned, they were allowed in.[8]

What would you do in such circumstances? Issue a snarky retort? Report the guard? Maybe call out the correctional facility on Twitter? Or worse, leave and not come back? Will mourned his reaction to the guard and wondered how he might have responded more compassionately. Reflecting on this encounter, David Dark wrote that Will urged him to look harder and more humbly at people he was tempted to dismiss, not to reduce a person to "the madness of a single moment."[9] Humble people don't judge others based on an isolated instance.

Just think how much good can be done through meekness. If we refused to reduce people to the madness of a single moment, Twitter might not exist! Interpersonal conflict would be tempered with gentleness and soul-searching. Parenting would be filled with more grace. Instead of snapping at my kids for not cleaning, I would tenderly investigate what happened and why my expectations weren't met. Meekness might prevent a wreck and promote peace at institutions of incarceration. By addressing inner pride, we can promote good outside ourselves. Will's story shows us the socially renewing power of humility, not only in his refusal to retaliate but also in his desire to put others first. It kept him, and others, serving the incarcerated.

Personally renewing humility. Humble people are attractive. We want to be around them, partly because they focus on us! They disappear as they ask us questions, sympathize with us, or celebrate things in our life. They anticipate our needs by cleaning the house, doing the dishes, or washing the car without being asked.

Humility really stands out when a person has a lot to brag about. I think of a friend of mine who has a PhD from Cambridge University, has published both academic and popular-level books, and drives a beat-up Corolla. When I'm with him, there's not a modicum of pretense, even when we're discussing subjects he is more knowledgeable about than I. He is kind enough to ask my opinion on things, and he speaks freely of his flaws. He is self-forgetful. I want to be more like him.

Jesus Christ is the supreme example of a great person with humility. He knew he was the eternal Son of God and possessed the power to create everything we know and do not know about. Yet he said things like "The Son of Man came not to be served but to serve, and to give his life as a ransom for many" (Matthew 20:28). He came to serve, give, and sacrifice for the eternal good of others. He said, "Blessed are the meek, for they shall inherit the earth" (Matthew 5:5). The word he used for *meek* shows up in another one of his sayings: "Take my yoke upon you, and learn from me, for I am gentle [meek] and lowly in heart, and you will find rest for your souls" (Matthew 11:29). Jesus' greatness didn't preclude him from serving others. In fact, it was a mark of his greatness.

Meekness is gentle in that it doesn't foist burdens on others or levy big expectations. It isn't quick to judge. Instead meekness bears burdens for others and removes expectations. Humility isn't just inviting; it's relieving. Jesus taught that we need more than physical relief. We need relief for our *souls*. Strong, weak, and middle pride are a heavy yoke attached to the self. They are burdensome attempts to secure worth. When Jesus tells us to take up our yoke, he's asking us to stop dragging the cargo of self-worth.

He wants us to stop trying to prove ourselves by gaining approval and applause, by standing on "our" truth. Instead he wants us to admit our sinful pride, receive forgiveness, and find our worth in him. He lived the life of humble obedience to God that we could never live and died the death we deserve so we can find rest for our soul. He extends acceptance and approval until our hearts are full. The icon of humility tells us there's no burden to carry and nothing to prove. "Just come and rest," he says. This is a lifelong lesson.

THE DIRECTION OF GRACE

The apostle Peter wasn't always a saint. A rough-and-tumble fisherman, he was boisterous, strong, and ambitious. And he had the chutzpah to correct Jesus. He even tried to prevent him from going to the cross: "And Peter took him aside and began to rebuke him, saying, 'Far be it from you, Lord! This shall never happen to you'" (Matthew 16:22). But Peter learned humility over time. While hiding in a courtyard, having denied any association with Jesus three times, he was humbled by the rooster's crow reminding him of his broken promise to never abandon his master. We too have denied Christ—the greatest and humblest of men, the Lion and the Lamb (Revelation 5:5-6). But we can also learn humility.

Years later the older, wiser Peter wrote, "Clothe yourselves, all of you, with humility toward one another, for 'God opposes the proud but gives grace to the humble.' Humble yourselves, therefore, under the mighty hand of God so that at the proper time he may exalt you" (1 Peter 5:5-6). Humility became a virtue for him.

So how did he get there? Notice that Peter said God opposes the proud. Strong pride puts us in opposition to God. It insists others look up in applause instead of dressing down in humility. Weak pride also opposes God because it demands approval from someone else. It also snubs Jesus in search of that approval. Middle pride replaces God altogether, locating approval and applause in a deified self. Peter reasoned that the proud can't enjoy grace, because we refuse to stand downstream from God. But grace flows down, not up, as we take in God's marvelous glory. To become truly humble, we have to look up at the glory.

All forms of pride seek a kind of glory. And not all of that is bad. In Hebrew, the word *glory* means "weight." Pride is an attempt to assign weight to ourselves. But humility recognizes the need for someone outside us to give us that weight. Paul explained that it comes from having "Christ in you, the hope of glory"

(Colossians 1:27). With Christ, the greatest and humblest of beings mystically indwelling us by faith, we don't have to assign ourselves weight. We don't have to conjure a lovely idea of the self. Instead a glory outside us comes to live in us: Christ in us, the hope of glory. Jesus secured this glory for us through his debt-paying death on the cross and his mighty resurrection: his injury for our reward, his obedience for our disobedience, his right-eousness for our unrighteousness. It hardly seems fair. That's grace!

With his heroic work done, we no longer have to imagine doing the things that others have done. Jesus pinned *his* medals to *our* chest. He assigned his glory to us (Colossians 3:11). Christ in you, not you in you, is the hope of glory. Ultimately, we need *his* truth not *our* truth. When we stand downstream of Jesus' glory, we receive a grace that lifts us up.

INHERITING THE WORLD

How do we cultivate humility? Two things are essential: a true view of self and a greater view of God. How do we get a true view of self? By practicing the first two Beatitudes: "Blessed are the poor in spirit" and "those who mourn" (Matthew 5:3, 4). The poor mourn sin and evil, asking God to show us our true selves, and confessing our sins to him. This humble act allows us to receive his forgiveness and enjoy his grace. It also expands our view of him and of the greatness of his grace.

Traditionally Christians practiced a rhythm of being poor in spirit both morning and evening. In the evening, while lying on a bed or sitting in a chair, they reflected on their sins and confessed them to the Father. In the morning, they rose to meet him, reading the Scriptures to take in a vista of his glory. This rhythm fostered an accurate view of themselves and a greater view of God.

We get a bigger vision of God by looking at him in Scripture, where he reveals his character and glory. If we fail to look at him, we grow bigger in our own eyes. And the longer we look at Christ, the more lovely he becomes. This is also true when we're attracted to another person. The more lovely she is, the more difficult it is to take our eyes off her. If we love her, we look her in the face. Similarly we need to slow down and linger over God's beauty and greatness. Look him in the face long enough to take in his glory.

To see more of God's greatness is to get in touch with who we truly are: his daughters and sons fashioned to worship him. Worship frees us from seeking glory for ourselves. Car karaoke to your favorite God-centered artists. Train your eyes on God by reading chapters of Scripture like Job 38–39 and 40–42, or by praying Solomon's Prayer (2 Chronicles 6). Or soak in the vision of our cosmic God in Isaiah 6. Read authors who are taken with the greatness of God, such as St. Augustine, John Calvin, William Perkins, Thomas Watson, Jonathan Edwards, J. I. Packer, and John Piper. Or simply go for a walk and look for his invisible attributes revealed in creation (Romans 1:20).

Practice Godward humility and you'll eventually inherit the world. The idea of this inheritance is taken directly from Psalm 37, which contains five variations of the same earth-inheriting promise (vv. 3, 9, 11, 22, 29). In each instance, the promise of inheriting the land is in the context of being oppressed and hurt by proud people. The land to come isn't merely a personal plot of paradise or a world where our name is in lights.

It's this world renewed. It's our earth deposed of evil by the returning Christ. In fact, the psalm says the wicked and proud will be cut off, their weapons turned on themselves (vv. 9, 10, 15). But the meek will enjoy peace (v. 11), abundance (v. 19), and justice as they dwell in the land (vv. 27-28).

This is the land of Christ, but the meek don't just inherit the earth; they inherit heaven too—a new heaven and a new earth. And the humbler we become, the more we get a taste of that land here and now. We get a foot in the door of the far-off country. As we humble ourselves under the mighty hand of God, he lifts us up in good time. With *this* as our inheritance, we have nothing to lose by being humble—and everything to gain.

OVERCOMING YOUR CHAOS

- ◆ Think about who you tend to compare yourself to in this season of life. How do you feel about yourself when you're making this comparison? What are you seeking through this comparison (approval, applause, self-actualization)?
- ◆ Confess to God how you are proud. Ask him to forgive you and to increase your awe of him and decrease your attention to yourself.
- ◆ What can Jesus offer you to replace what you're looking for in pride?
- ◆ Pick a passage of Scripture that describes the greatness of God. Meditate on it over the next week, looking for all the ways God is great. Praise him for those things.
- ◆ How could humility change the way you respond to people who hold different views than you?

Five

RIGHTEOUSNESS IN AN AGE OF VALUES

"Blessed are those who hunger and thirst for righteousness, for they shall be satisfied."

MATTHEW 5:6

I N THE CRITIC-ADORED FILM UPGRADE, Grey Trace receives an AI implant that enhances his reflexes, strength, and intellect. He moves like a souped-up Jason Bourne, effectively taking down bad guys. But when his AI gets shut down, he loses his superhuman abilities. So Grey searches for a hacker to reboot it. After he finds the hacker, he asks if "she" will do a job for him. The hacker retorts, "Yeah, but why do you have to be so binary?"

Then the camera pans out so the viewer can see "she" is androgynous. A nonbinary hacker—ironic for a person whose livelihood relies on a binary code of ones and zeroes. The film raises moral tensions over and over again. We can't really escape binaries: male and female, righteous and wicked, right and wrong, ones and zeros. We live in a moral universe.

Our knee-jerk reaction to the hacker scene reflects our moral sensibilities. If we believe gender is based on biology, we respond one way, and if we believe gender is socially constructed, we respond in another. We either approve or disapprove of binary gender.

The plot of the film twists and turns around moral dilemmas. In the opening scene, the Trace's self-driving car is hacked and rerouted to a desolate parking lot. When they get out, his wife is assaulted, and he takes a shot to the back. Paralyzed, he helplessly watches his wife struggle to escape. Suddenly she's shot to death and collapses to the ground. Their eyes meet as the light fades from her eyes. Grey passes out.

When he awakes, he discovers he no longer has use of his arms and legs. Wheelchair-bound and quadriplegic, Grey spins into despair. But once he receives the AI implant, he sets out to secure justice by righting the wrong.

The story is driven by a moral imperative: criminals must be brought to justice. But competing visions of justice are put to the test. The film poses ethical questions all the way through. Will the cops do their job? Is it right for Grey to alter his body with an AI implant? Should he use his enhanced abilities to act as a vigilante? The viewer is forced to decide which choices are right.

Even if we don't like binaries, at some level we operate in them. We want the film to reflect *our* view, for the court to come down in favor of *our* perspective and the world to side with *us*. We, of course, hold the "right" view.

All those social-media rants? Binary convictions. We can't escape morality. Deep down, we know righteous and wicked, good and evil, are real categories.

Despite the fact that we live in a moral universe, most of us don't walk around thinking we're righteous or wicked. We may think, *I've probably done some righteous things and maybe some wicked stuff, but I don't fit into either category. I'm somewhere in-between, and honestly, I wouldn't even use those words: righteous and wicked.*

VALUES INSTEAD OF VIRTUES

We live in an age increasingly uncomfortable with tight moral categories. Instead of speaking about what we "believe is right," we may say, "That doesn't line up with my values." Morally ambivalent, we often hesitate to take a stand. Say an ethical issue comes up at work: someone gossips about a coworker, your boss asks you to exaggerate the numbers, or you notice the tardiness of a friend. Do you confront the gossip and stand up for your coworker? Do you take an honest stand and refuse to go along with your boss? Do you check in on your coworker to see if everything is okay and, if so, encourage him to arrive on time? If not, why?

Because we lack moral courage.

When moral ambivalence begins to fill a society, it results in what C. S. Lewis described as "men without chests," people who lack conviction and moral fiber.[1] This grotesque, emasculating image is meant to rattle the moral imagination. Yet often we can't imagine taking a stand, because we've been captivated by something else: the subjective values of the self.

The modern self prefers values over virtues. Transparency, kindness, and authenticity are preferred over honesty, goodness, and truth. Core values are often plastered on the walls in company common areas, listed on product labels, and bulleted on church websites. Values drive success, but virtues forge character. Virtues are firm; values are soft and mushy. We may say we value family, while we lie about a porn addiction. We may boast about community, while rarely practicing hospitality. We may say we value church without lifting a finger to serve others. What good is a value when it is so easily ignored?

A journalist visited a trendy Silicon Valley startup that listed transparency as one of its core values. While there, he discovered the company was two to three months away from running out of funding. When the journalist asked the CEO how the company's employees felt about being almost out of funding, the CEO responded, "Well, they would never know that." Shouldn't the employees know their jobs are on the line? What happened to the value of transparency? Values are so soft; they can be molded to our liking. They conveniently support and express the preference of the self—or in this case, "the company." Values don't require strict adherence, but stodgy, old honesty insists on the truth.

Virtue replacement. The gradual slide into values away from virtues can reach a point of virtue replacement. In a Delta Air Lines commercial, the viewer follows a camera through gorgeous footage from more than fifteen destinations across the globe, then hears this announcement: "The old saying 'Good things come to those who wait' is just that—old. Good things come to those who go." While inspiring us to explore the world (and buy a ticket), Delta subtly replaces an "old" virtue with a new value. Out with patience—and those who wait—and in with the impatiently ambitious. The ad urges us to "get out there and chase" good things, which are depicted as experience, wealth, fine food, and stunning settings. It doesn't advocate chasing down humility, patience, righteousness, or service to the poor.

Now, don't get me wrong; I love travel. I've found it to be very educational, and it inspires appreciation for other cultures. And I don't expect an airline to advertise the Beatitudes. However, two things are concerning about this ad. First, it blatantly dismisses a classic, self-effacing virtue (patience) by casting it aside as "old" and implying a "new" value is better. But is newer better? Second, the replacement value appeals to the self-aggrandizing ambition to get out there and grab whatever we want. Call it drive, ambition, or passion, but beneath the words is an appeal to what one philosopher calls "finding satisfaction in the lovely Idea of ourselves." In this ad, the lovely idea is impatiently running after an adventurous, experienced self rather than a humble, patient self. Self-made values subvert transcendental virtues.

A MORAL VACUUM

Virtue replacement creates a moral vacuum. In a vacuum, we reach out for *something* to hold onto. We need it to make us feel secure or successful. One trend is to grasp community service. Cultural commentator David Brooks writes, "Today, community service is sometimes used as a patch to cover over inarticulateness about the inner life. . . . We tend to convert moral questions into resource-allocation questions."[2] This is evident when businesses are asked about how they promote character. They often respond by discussing philanthropy. When schools are asked how they instill virtues, they present their adopt-a-highway cleanup initiative.

Peter Wood, president of the National Association of Scholars, asserts that colleges and universities are now expected "to engage in the pursuit of social justice more than they need to pursue command of particular subjects or general knowledge."[3] This expectation often carries over into perceptions of the church, where pastors are expected to behave as activists, worship services are required to advertise individual causes, and social and political action often matter more than personal holiness. The old virtues of chastity and honesty are less important in the church than they once were. One need only think of the Catholic sex-abuse scandals and evangelical veneration of Donald Trump, who, according to a *Washington Post* article, lied 2,140 times in his first year in office.[4] In sum, when asked about virtue, people often think of a value—hard work, transparency, community, social action. But rarely do humility, patience, and truthfulness spring to mind.

The atrophying effects of virtue replacement create a societal need for moral guidance. Where should we look? Surely what's often called "the greatest moral document of all time" would be a good place to start? Yet many can't name a Beatitude, much less one of the Ten Commandments.

During Jay Leno's final episode as host of *The Tonight Show*, he asked people on the street to name one of the Ten

Commandments. The first to respond said, "Freedom of speech!" Another said, "God helps those who help themselves." Not a single interviewee could name a commandment. We are in an age characterized by what Christian philosopher Dallas Willard called "the disappearance of moral knowledge."

In his posthumously published book, *The Disappearance of Moral Knowledge*, Willard reviewed developments in ethical theory over the last two centuries and concluded: "The disappearance of moral knowledge, in the manner reviewed, is not an expression of truth rationally secured, but is the outcome of an historical drift, with no rational justification at all or only the thinnest show of one."[5] The disappearance of moral knowledge was not the result of public discourse in which we weighed arguments and established facts. It simply happened, creeping over us like an early-morning fog. In other words, there aren't good reasons for our good crisis.

MORALITY WITHOUT GOD

Can we find good reasons to be righteous? In 1896, George Jacob Holyoake, an atheist and coiner of the term *secularism*, insisted it's possible to do good apart from God, saying, "It is good to do good."[6] What good was he referring to? Reflecting on what *good* is for secularists, sociologist Phil Zuckerman said, "The answer is simple: the Golden Rule. Being good means treating others as you would like to be treated. That is the bedrock of secular morality."[7] It's undoubtedly good to treat others as we would like to be treated, and in general that can promote ethical behavior. However, unbeknownst to Zuckerman, the Golden Rule is taken from the Sermon on the Mount: "So whatever you wish that others would do to you, do also to them, for this is the Law and the Prophets" (Matthew 7:12). When appealing to the Golden Rule, secularists sometimes end up borrowing moral vocabulary and principles from Jesus and the Bible.

However, not all secularists appeal to the Golden Rule for their moral reasoning. Many appeal to some version of the adage "I am free to do whatever I like, as long as it doesn't hurt anybody." While this sounds good in theory, the problem with this "harm principle" is that not all notions of harm are the same. One person may consider watching pornography an innocuous act, unharmful to anyone, saying, "What I do in the privacy of my home is my business." However, another person says pornography contributes to sexist attitudes, the exploitation of women, and sex trafficking.

Whose understanding of harm should we heed? To one person, watching porn is harmful to others. To another, it isn't harmful at all. If we decide to honor the part of the population that wants to watch porn, we harm those who are exploited. If we support a crackdown on sex trafficking, we harm the porn industry and the individual's right to view pornography. The harm principle is inadequate for determining what is good. We need a moral norm to determine what is harmful and what is not.[8]

COMMENDING RIGHTEOUSNESS

In the Bible, Noah is the first person described as righteous: "Noah was a righteous man, blameless in his generation. Noah walked with God" (Genesis 6:9). The Hebrew word for righteous, *tsaddiq*, means to be morally in the right. Noah was a man of remarkable faith who constructed an ark when no water was in sight. But he also got drunk after the flood and passed out, exposing himself. How, then, could Noah be described as righteous—"blameless," no less?

I've heard some fantastical explanations that try to resolve this dilemma. For example, the postflood climate was so drastically different from the preflood climate that it was easier to get drunk. In addition to being outlandish, this explanation is speculative. How could God sanction a description of Noah as righteous?

The psalms repeatedly describe God as righteous:

For the LORD is righteous;
he loves righteous deeds;
the upright shall behold his face. (Psalm 11:7;
    see also 145:17)

Psalm 11 shows us several important things about righteousness: the Lord is inherently righteous; he delights when righteousness is expressed in his creation; and righteousness originates with him. If righteousness is original to Yahweh, this uniquely qualifies him to determine what is righteous.

Yahweh sees Noah as righteous. Somehow Noah met God's moral standard. Since we know Noah sinned, his description as righteous can't imply sinless perfection, nor can it convey blanket approval of Noah's every action. What then does God mean when he calls Noah righteous? It means God sees *the whole* of Noah's life and concludes he was righteous. Similarly, when we say "He's a great guy" we don't mean everything a person does is great. Instead, we mean all things being said, he's generally a good person.

The word *blameless* is sometimes translated as *whole* or *complete*. This description of Noah is a commentary on the *wholeness* of his life, not on his every action. Noah lived a whole life. How? By obeying God's will, choosing to do what was right, and preferring good over evil in contrast to those around him. Not flawlessly but consistently. How did Noah do it? Noah walked with God. It was closeness to God that produced his moral rectitude. Noah took on the qualities of his Creator. This kind of life brings a satisfaction all its own.

I've heard people compare a life of righteousness to taking a pill every day. As long as you take it, you enjoy the effects of moral goodness: contentment, peace, joy. But when you skip the pill, the effects of your immoral choices take hold of you. They disrupt the contentment flowing through you. There is a jarring difference between a righteous life and an unrighteous life.

John came to faith in Jesus in his late fifties. Prior to meeting Jesus, he believed something like this: "There is no right or wrong. There is only neutral. Some things work out better; other things work out worse. But we're not bound to any code. There's no such thing as sin." But his choices caught up with him. His promiscuity led to a messy divorce and estrangement from his adult children. He struggled in his second marriage and realized he needed help. Eventually he turned to Christ for forgiveness and new life, and he began walking with God.

As God rubbed off on John, he began to interpret his prior moral views differently. Then, at a men's retreat, reflecting on his pre-Christian life, he said, "I'm fifty-five years old. I lived fifty-four of those years in sin. I thought my moral decisions didn't matter, but they do. I thought it was fun and satisfying to be in an open marriage, but things came crashing down. If you think living how you want is the way to go, you're wrong. If you don't think moral decisions matter, come talk to me. I can tell you; believe me, morality matters."

Now John is reaping the benefits of a righteous life—not a perfect life. He walks with God, bears the fruit of the Spirit, and talks about how satisfying life is when he's walking closely with God. Like Noah, John is learning to enjoy the benefits of walking righteously.

Living a righteous life ushers in wholeness. It lines us up with God issuing a host of virtues, such as humility, purity, mercy, love, and endurance. This is why each Beatitude starts with the word *blessed*. The blessing that ensues from a life of righteousness is the result of living how our Creator intended us to live. He has designed us for flourishing, which happens when we align ourselves with his design. Righteousness is moral goodness that takes its cues from God. This righteousness isn't purely individualistic. It can't contain itself; it spills over into society, touching lives around us. So while righteousness is personally satisfying, it is also socially renewing.

PUBLIC AND PERSONAL RIGHTEOUSNESS

Martin Luther King Jr. thundered, "No, no, we are not satisfied, and we will not be satisfied until justice rolls down like waters, and righteousness like a mighty stream." He called on the biblical virtue of righteousness found in Amos 5:24 to advance racial justice for African Americans.

In the original context, Amos was redressing Israel's moral and social failure. They abhorred the truth and trampled the poor, greedily sought comfort while extorting the oppressed. In response, he called upon God to bring about both public and personal righteousness.

Psalm 17 also calls upon God for righteousness. Surrounded by violent men and suffering slurs, King David implored God, "Hear a just [*tsaddiq*] cause, O LORD; attend to my cry!" (v. 1). He used *tsaddiq* to cry for *justice* in society. The ousted king asked God to put things right. He described the wicked in relation to the righteous: they "close their hearts to pity" and are "lurking in ambush" (vv. 10, 12). David, too, confidently calls upon God to act, "Arise, O LORD! Confront him, subdue him" (v. 13). In his pursuit of justice, David banks on God's righteous character. He also appeals to the Lord as a Savior to those in need of refuge (v. 7). Through David's plea, we see that righteousness is social not just personal. A righteous person takes up the cause of the oppressed and contends for justice.

Yet David resolved not to take part in their wickedness. While seeking social justice, David put his ultimate hope not in justice as he saw it but how God distributes it. He concluded, "As for me, I shall behold your face in righteousness; / when I awake, I shall be satisfied with your likeness" (v. 15). Regardless of how God answered his prayer, David was determined to seek God for satisfaction. He resolved to rivet his attention not on the unjust circumstances but on God's righteous face. He acknowledged injustice and sought justice but did so before the face of God. Theologian Nancy deClaisse-Walford commented that David "closes his eyes in the trusting confidence that the new day will dawn with hope—because all tomorrows are in the hands of the Lord."[9] More than seeking social justice, David determined to trust his tomorrows to God. He trusted God's righteous character and was satisfied with *his* providence and *his* timing, knowing the Lord is good.

This psalm reveals a connection between God's righteous character and holy justice. Because God is righteous, he will uphold justice. This promotes both personal and social righteousness. However, the psalm also reveals a connection between righteous character and the pursuit of justice. Out of his flawless, righteous character, God determines what is just and *when* justice is achieved. We must learn to accept his providential justice, as difficult as it may be, and trust his character to work it out in the world. This is easier said than done.

All of us are prone to replace God with our own vision of justice. This can tyrannize both social justice advocates and those who are indifferent to justice. The advocate can be so dominated by the "god" of justice that failure to achieve just policies, treatment, and ends leads to self-destructive anger or despair. When enslaved to the god of justice, it's easy to judge those who disagree with us or those who are slow to grasp the gravity of the issue. This functional god leads to divisiveness and disunity. Alternatively the person who insists on being treated fairly (personal justice) but doesn't seek to extend fair treatment to others (social justice) snubs those in real need. Failure to advocate for social justice is a failure to embrace the character of God. Moreover, it becomes oppressive to those who are in need of social righteousness. Writing off social justice is insensitive, demeaning, and downright ungodly.

This dual tyranny reveals the need for something more than *our* grasp of justice. Were we to receive *divine* justice, we would all be reduced to smoldering wicks. No one is righteous, not even one, apart from Jesus (Romans 3:10). Like God, we need to hold personal and social righteousness together. We need to cultivate righteous character that promotes patience, humility, and love while we also advocate for social justice that upholds the cause of the minority, the orphan, the homeless, and the disabled. Above all, we should seek the righteous face of God which beams with unimpeachable justice and satisfying goodness. As David concluded, "As for me, I shall behold your face in righteousness; / when I awake, I shall be satisfied with your likeness" (Psalm 17:15).

Returning to Jesus' Beatitude, when he calls us to pursue righteousness, he doesn't drive a wedge between personal and public good. Instead he promises flourishing to those who seek both. God calls us to a righteousness that is strong and dependable, like an oak, not waify and flexible like the subjective self. True righteousness is attractive and grounding. People of character exude a humble righteousness that's inspiring and helpful to others. But most of all, true righteousness glorifies God, not us.

RIGHTEOUS TOGETHER

No one can perfectly fulfill this Beatitude, much less the entire Sermon on the Mount. In some cases, churches are even obstacles to the moral teaching of Jesus. Because of this, a message on the cover of a *Newsweek* magazine recommended we "forget the church, follow Jesus." The lead article identified a crisis in

Christianity that makes it barely recognizable: it is selectively moral, highly politicized, and dominated by a focus on self-help and prosperity. A scathing indictment, indeed.

The author of the article, Andrew Sullivan, went on to argue that the essence of Christianity is not its complex doctrines, the cross of Christ, or his sufferings but how Jesus conducted himself. "The point was how he conducted himself through it all—calm, loving, accepting, radically surrendering even the basic control of his own body and telling us that this was what it means to truly transcend our world and be with God."[10] He has a point: Christians should look more like Christ.

However, the same critique can be leveled at Sullivan and churches who adopt his characterization of Christianity. Sullivan is not "accepting" of some of the moral teachings of Jesus, insisting Jesus never spoke about homosexuality or abortion. His assertion reflects a superficial reading of Jesus who soundly condemned all sexual sin (Matthew 5:27-30) and murder (5:21-22), which can include homosexuality and abortion.[11]

More to the point, Jesus' ultimate goal was not to provide a moral example but to bear the cross and embrace resurrection in order to forgive and reconcile all our immoralities and sins, for "the Son of Man must suffer many things and be rejected by the elders and chief priests and scribes, and be killed, and on the third day be raised" (Luke 9:22; see also 9:44; 18:31-33; 24:25-27). And St. Paul reminds us, if Christ has not been raised, we are still in our sins (1 Corinthians 15:17). We can't pick and choose the teachings of Christ we want to keep. Nor can we reduce Jesus to the poster child of our pet moralities or political persuasions. Rather, the collective weight of *all* of Jesus' teachings should drive us to Christ to find forgiveness and power to live moral lives that please God, regardless of how unpopular they may be. We cannot do this alone.

While critical of the flaws of the church, Gary Gutting, professor of philosophy at University of Notre Dame, takes a more balanced approach to the role of churches in addressing the moral crisis: "These churches have also been central in sustaining the traditions of thought and practice that transformed Jesus' passionate but enigmatic teachings into coherent and fruitful moral visions. They have been the air—however polluted—that has fed the fire of his message."[12] The solution is not to forget the church. Rather, the church is meant to be an alternative community that embodies Jesus' moral vision—a city on a hill that glows not with our perfection but his.

We are meant to be righteous together.

One afternoon I met a skeptical young man for coffee at a coffee shop downtown. He shared how he had been disappointed and hurt by churches. As I listened, I sympathized with his pain and extended an apology. Then he leaned forward and asked, "Will your church disappoint me too?" I thought about his question for a few seconds before responding, "Yes, we will disappoint you, but we will do our best to consistently point you to a Savior who does not disappoint." This is the beauty and the power of the church—an imperfect people pointing one another to a perfect Christ, being perfected by his Spirit over time. I invited him to join us in being perfected by God together.

There are many evidences of Jesus' fruitful moral vision beaming through the church, from William Wilberforce's long labor to overturn slavery in Britain to Gary Haugen's work with

International Justice Mission—and all the churches that partner with it—to rescue victims of human trafficking. In addition, there are the everyday moral successes of people and communities that quietly practice the Beatitudes of Christ, enriching the lives of those around them.

Gutting insists there is no Sermon on the Mount *without* the church. This brings to mind our observation about the kingdom of God in chapter two: the kingdom comes to earth *communally*, where the reign of God is made visible in those who seek to fulfill Jesus' moral vision together. We can't actually practice the Beatitudes in isolation. Patience, humility, righteousness, and love require a community, whether you are Christian or not. But in the church, we gain not only a community to be righteous with but also a power to be righteous by—the Spirit of God. The Spirit incrementally transforms the church, as the church in turn enriches its surrounding communities. Jesus called the church to be the kindling, and the Spirit the oxygen, to the fire of his message. We are meant to be righteous together.

HUNGER AND THIRST

How do we pursue righteousness?

Should we tally our moral successes next to our moral failures, striving for our successes to outnumber failures? We simply lack the omniscience and humility to compile an accurate tally. What then should we do? Jesus said we are to "hunger and thirst" for it (Matthew 5:6).

Hunger and thirst aren't optional in life; they're essential. We're so dependent on eating and drinking that an internal notification goes off every few hours. As a result, we eat multiple meals a day. If we didn't have hunger and thirst, we wouldn't eat or drink, and we'd eventually die. Hunger is *vital* to life. So it is with spiritual life. If we don't hunger and thirst for righteousness, our soul will shrivel up. But we don't always sense the spiritual signals for righteousness. We may not "feel" hungry.

Hunger and thirst are also *painful*. They aren't comfortable sensations. Think about how your stomach growls and gnaws as lunch approaches or about a dry-throated heave after a run. If we need to awaken hunger, we may have to force ourselves to be around food. This can be hard if you're spiritually starved. Like anorexics who have to force themselves to eat, we may have to discipline ourselves to consume what's good for us. You may need to set the alarm clock earlier to get up and commune with God. Or you might need to slow down to admire character in others, open the Bible and observe God's righteousness, and practice a spirit of prayerfulness throughout the day. It may be hard to slow down, sit still, and meditate on God's Word, but through these disciplines we absorb righteousness!

In Christian circles there is an odd idea that going to church services or being around other Christians will somehow produce more character, as if virtue comes through osmosis. This is like believing that attending entrepreneurial conferences and hanging out with entrepreneurs produces a successful startup. But we know it doesn't. We have to roll up our sleeves and do the hard work. Accept the pain, embrace the discipline, and get to work. We often plan our meals and our work, but do we have a plan for our character? Consider starting and ending your day with fifteen minutes of prayer and reflection on the God of righteousness. Start or join a group of people who are serious about hungering and thirsting for righteousness. Read a book about holiness, or apply this book with others by doing the *Ordering Your Moral Chaos* section together. Hunger growls. Thirst can burn. But both prompt satisfaction: "Blessed are those who hunger and thirst for righteousness, for they will be satisfied."

Against my natural desires, I went on a diet that removed carbs and sugars; I ate primarily vegetables and protein for weeks. When I decided to treat myself to a dessert the first time, I sank my teeth into a moist cookie—and I was incredibly disappointed. The sugar tasted synthetic, impure because my taste buds had acclimated to a better diet. My hunger and thirst had been clarified, enabling me to enjoy natural sugars in fruit. Eliminating processed foods awakened my appetite to flavor, dazzling my taste buds.

Similarly spiritual hunger creates moral *clarity*. You begin to *enjoy* righteousness. It awakens you to a longing for God and his work in the world. You're seized by the richness of Scripture, the urgency of holiness, and the importance of justice. When you change your diet from values to virtues and hunger and thirst for righteousness, you'll find your tastes awaken to the sublime presence of God. You become more deeply satisfied than you could have imagined.

Andy Warhol was far from what most would consider righteous. His art studio, The Factory, was a center for the pop art movement and all the moral excesses that went along with it. However, a closer look at Warhol's life reveals that religion kept him from going over the edge. He prayed daily, frequently attended Mass, and spent holidays volunteering at a soup kitchen, where he befriended the homeless and poor. He even put his nephew through seminary. When openly gay Warhol refused to support the gay rights movement, his friends blamed his faith.

In the final year of his life, he became obsessed with Da Vinci's *The Last Supper*. He produced variations of the painting with pop icons stamped over them, the ordinary obscuring the extraordinary. Reflecting on this artistic choice, editor of the *Catholic Herald*, Michael Davis, comments, "The implication is that our appetites distract us from the vision of Christ."[13]

What appetites are distracting you from Jesus? What might you need to fast from to awaken longing for righteousness? What new habits do you need to form? If a measure of religious discipline restrained Warhol and promoted some good in his life, then surely we should heed the message of his closing piece and train our appetites with a vision of Christ.

OVERCOMING YOUR CHAOS

- ◆ In a moral vacuum, we often hold on to something for support. What do you tend to hold on to: an individual value, a replacement virtue? Be specific.

- ◆ How could your imbalanced focus on a value or virtue negatively affect others? What can you do to rectify this?

- ◆ Identify a next step toward growing in righteousness "together." Share it with a friend, and ask him or her to encourage you in it.

- ◆ What self-righteousness do you need to confess to God? To your community?

- How is Jesus' righteousness better than our righteousness? How can you humbly keep Jesus' performance—not your own or others'—in view?
- What hunger pangs do you need to embrace in order to hunger and thirst for righteousness?

Six

MERCY IN AN AGE OF TOLERANCE

*"Blessed are the merciful, for
they shall receive mercy."*

MATTHEW 5:7

I F YOU'RE STARTING TO FEEL overwhelmed by the Beatitudes, you're not alone. When I consider the call to be poor in spirit, to mourn evil and sin, to walk humbly, and to hunger and thirst for righteousness, I wonder, *Is this even possible?* I'm tempted to throw up my hands and give up. Or I find myself inspired to double down to make significant changes and strive for more. But then I catch myself patting myself on the back. Mercy is just what I need. Or is it?

THIN MERCY

Driving along my usual route from the house I saw red and blue lights swirling in my rearview mirror. *Surely those aren't for me?*

I was going only a few miles an hour over the speed limit. The police car stayed on my tail. As I pulled into a neighborhood, I immediately started praying, "Please don't let the officer give me a ticket. I know I probably deserve it, but money is tight. Maybe he'll give me a warning?" I asked God for mercy.

A thin understanding of mercy misconstrues it as "overlooking a wrong" or "not being so judgmental." When an officer issues a warning citation, however, he doesn't overlook a wrong; he reinforces it. The pink slip is there to remind us *we are wrong*; we *deserve* the ticket; we broke the law. Mercy exists because of justice. Although we deserve justice (a ticket), when we get what we don't deserve (a warning)—that's mercy! Unfortunately I got justice.

Mercy can't exist without judgment. If the law doesn't exist, there's no warning citation. If there is no standard for right and wrong, there's no wrong to forgive. This kind of moral clarity can be uncomfortable, even humbling. We'd much rather impugn the cop or make an excuse about the speed limit to avoid being wrong.

THE JUDGMENT OF TOLERANCE

Most of us don't like to think of ourselves as recipients of mercy. For this reason, tolerance can be quite appealing. It smooths blunt moral edges so we don't have to admit failure.

Tolerance props up the Big Me.

The impulse of tolerance is to overlook a wrong, tolerate what's unjust, wink an eye at what's immoral.[1] It's thin mercy, not real mercy. This impulse flows from its chief aim: to validate the individual, not what is just. Tolerance makes a secret pact:

If you accept whatever works for me, I'll accept whatever works for you. Right and wrong don't matter as much as getting our way. This policy of tolerance operates under the guise of accepting other's views, beliefs, and decisions. In reality, tolerance rejects any view that opposes it. It tries to sacrifice judgment on the altar of inclusivity, but in the process, it excludes any who oppose it.

Consider how tolerance works in the gender-neutral bathroom debate. Tolerance says, "Make bathrooms neutral so transgender and transsexual people are comfortable going to whichever bathroom they prefer." A mother and her young daughter go to the bathroom and discover a transgender male is in it. Concerned about what her daughter will see, the mother does an about-face and ushers her daughter out of the bathroom. She reports this to the store manager who, in response, asks her to be more tolerant.

Now, isn't tolerance accepting *anyone's* view? Why should the mother have to give up her view? Why isn't her preference to go to the bathroom with her daughter without a sexed male in the room valid? The tolerant manager is being intolerant of the mother and daughter.

Even tolerance has a standard. In this case, it insists on a progressive view of gender while dismissing the traditional view. Tolerance is quite judgmental. It holds people to its own assumption of what is right and wrong—and it even insists on it. On this particular issue, the "tolerant" perspective has tried to enforce its view by lobbying to legalize gender-neutral bathrooms. Why shouldn't the mother and daughter be free to use a bathroom without the other sex in the room? Who's to say what's right and what's wrong? Tolerance is uneven in its judgments and often quite blind to this moral dilemma.

Planet Fitness boasts a "judgment-free zone" so anyone can work out without the fear of being judged. The gym works hard to keep bodybuilders out so others don't have to feel inferior about their body. I like the idea, but it's not very tolerant. If Planet Fitness were really "judgment-free," it would allow anyone in, including bodybuilders, gym rats, and meatheads.

Thirty-four-year-old Eric Stagno of Haverhill, Massachusetts, decided to put the judgment-free zone to the test. He walked into a Planet Fitness and stripped naked at the front desk, walked back and forth to stretch, checked himself out in the mirror, and then started doing yoga on the mats. A staff person promptly called the police, and Stagno was arrested for indecent exposure. When interviewed about Stagno, the officer said, "The only comment he made was that he thought it was a judgment-free zone." The cops had a good laugh, and the news anchor commented, "A judgment-free zone but not clothing-free zone. Stagno was handcuffed in the buff."[2] In a funny yet disgusting way, Stagno had exposed a weakness in tolerance. Tolerance is not judgment-free!

WHAT IS JUSTICE?

If we can't keep from making judgments, wouldn't it make sense to figure out how to make the *best* judgments? If we hone in on what is just, we can be more equitable and more merciful people. Where, then, does justice come from?

Plato witnessed a rise in injustice and a decline in democracy in Athens. Motivated by the crumbling foundations of his own society and the death of his mentor, Socrates, he set out to formulate justice in *The Republic*. The result was foundational for Western civilization.

In *The Republic*, Plato engaged in an extended debate with his contemporaries over the nature of justice. His primary critique of his contemporaries was that they believed justice to be external to humanity, something humankind must *do* or accomplish. No doubt he would level a similar critique of the social justice movement today. Justice isn't just something we do; it's something we are. In contrast to an externally focused, action-based understanding of justice, Plato argued that justice is internal. He believed a just soul leads to a just life, which in turn promotes a just society. It is the *just soul* that transforms society. He retorted, "Then the just soul and the just man will live well, and the unjust man will live ill?" Was Plato correct in reasoning that justice is rooted in something internal, something we are? Or is justice external, based on things we do or do not do?

Despite Plato's considerable influence, his notion of justice differs considerably from our practice of justice in American liberal democracy. We actually conceive of justice quite differently. Philosopher Chris Wright points out that Plato's conception of justice is based on hierarchy—something liberal democracy often shuns. We reserve the right to rebel, to upset order, and to challenge the state based on our commitment to *individual freedom*. While freedom of speech and assembly are wonderful rights guaranteed by the Constitution and Bill of Rights, these freedoms should not trump federal law. National law governs individual rights for the collective good. However, while justice is inscribed on our federal buildings, individual freedom is perhaps the flag that flies highest in our land.

To the contrary, Plato maintained that the collective good was more important than individual freedom. Wright says, "Plato's concept of justice is instead inspired by his conviction that the collective takes ethical precedence over the individual, that there is a cosmic order into which each person is supposed to fit, and that virtue, and to an extent duty, is far more important than rights."[3] Americans share no such commitment to cosmic order and hierarchy. Now more than ever, the ordering principle of our ethics is the freedom of the individual. We rarely embrace cosmic or communal constraints on our freedom. Individual freedom, above all, must not be encroached upon.

Say you're on vacation in Athens, taking pictures of the Colosseum with your new iPhone. As you hold the phone up to take a picture of your friend in portrait mode, someone runs by and snatches your phone. You yell after her, but it's too late; she disappears into the densely packed cobblestone courtyard. Why was stealing your iPhone wrong? Americans tend to say it was wrong because an individual's right of ownership was transgressed. I have a right to my phone. But Plato would say the theft was wrong because it transgressed the cosmic order and disrupted the social good. Theft creates social unrest. In the former perspective, stealing transgresses the individual, but in the latter, theft transgresses the order of the cosmos and the welfare of the community. Which is better?

If justice is measured by respecting individual rights, the meaning of what is just can change from individual to individual. It follows that mercy also lacks consistency. Instead of being firm, it becomes thin, devolving into "random acts of kindness" dispensed at individual whim. However, if justice is cosmic order, then it is static, and our being merciful is a reflection of something greater than ourselves. So while Plato argues that virtues, like justice, are expressed in the soul, he ultimately locates them in the state governed by philosopher-kings. Although he envisioned the philosopher-kings as virtuous and reasonable people, the problem with relying on them is the same problem we encounter in relying on elected officials: both philosopher-kings and elected officials are flawed. While the state and its rulers have an important role to play, where does their collective vision for justice come from?

Which state adequately embodies justice? How do we know if a soul is truly just? It would seem we need a transcendental, universal origin for justice. Plato's eternal ideal of the Forms grounds and elevates his concept of justice by giving it an eternal cosmic-ness or universality. While justice fits nicely within the framework of the Forms, something as relational as mercy does not. Moreover, if justice and mercy are not only eternal but also personal, expressed supremely through people and societies, how can something as impersonal as a Form account for mercy? On this question, we must reach back to the Hebrews.

FOUNDATIONS FOR JUSTICE AND MERCY

Long before Plato and Aristotle, the Hebrews encountered a God named I AM, or Yahweh (Exodus 3:14). The name is a form of the Hebrew "to be" and can also be translated "I will be." When Moses was on the run from the Egyptian totalitarian state, he encountered this God. Interestingly, unlike Egyptian and Mesopotamian gods, I AM isn't associated with a parent god and isn't the result of primordial feuds. Instead he simply and quite profoundly *is*.

We often identify ourselves by our last name, a name that indicates what family we come from and that can be traced to learn more about our ancestry. I AM has no ancestry; he simply is. Yahweh is the self-referential and self-sustaining God. His name also transcends time and place. The psalm writer says,

> Before the mountains were brought forth,
>> or ever you had formed the earth and the world,
>> from everlasting to everlasting you are God.
> (Psalm 90:2)

I AM is transcendent and eternal, making him a logical and consistent source for justice.

Yahweh revealed more of his identity when he gave Moses the Ten Commandments. The very fact that Yahweh imparted a law reveals his orientation to justice. The commandments form a basis for judgment: don't commit adultery, murder, and so on. But he revealed even more. As Moses received the Ten Commandments, I AM descended upon Mount Sinai in a cloud of glory, accompanied by lightning and thunder, and proclaiming,

> The LORD, the LORD, a God merciful and gracious, slow to anger, and abounding in steadfast love and faithfulness, keeping steadfast love for thousands, forgiving iniquity and transgression and sin, but who will by no means clear the guilty, visiting the iniquity of the fathers on the children

and the children's children, to the third and the fourth generation. (Exodus 34:6-7)

What does this momentous event tell us?

The name I AM reveals two essential character traits: he is merciful and he is just. He forgives but does not clear the guilty. These character traits reveal an eternal, cosmic foundation for mercy and justice. They aren't ideals wished into existence out of thin air. Nor are they simply the state of certain souls or activities. Mercy and justice transcend the internal/external debate because they are *eternal* qualities of a self-referential, personal God. For this reason, they are part of the architecture of reality.

These virtues arise from the infinite space and eternal personality of God himself and, through his creation, enter our world. In the words of English professor Karen Swallow Prior, "Justice is less like finite land and more like the wildflowers that grow there, continually spreading as they bloom and re-seed themselves. Justice—like beauty—is rooted in infinity."[4] Thus the infinite and eternal God is a more reliable yet personal foundation for both justice and mercy.

THE UNIQUENESS OF THE PREACHER

With these foundational virtues in place, we can return to the Sermon on the Mount, where the I AM reveals himself in two ways that further illuminate mercy and justice. First, Jesus came as the I AM in the flesh. In his repeated "I AM" statements in the Gospel of John, Jesus aligns himself with Yahweh: "I am the light of the world. Whoever follows me will not walk in darkness, but will have the light of life" (John 8:12). Jesus shares in the glorious, ontological light of the Father. He further confides in his disciples, "Whoever has seen me has seen the Father" (John 14:9). This means Jesus shares in all the qualities of Yahweh, including his eternal mercy and justice. The preacher of the greatest moral document of all time is, in fact, I AM.

Second, as the I AM incarnate, Jesus extends mercy to us before returning to exact justice. He said to the Jews, "I told you that you would die in your sins, for unless you believe that I am he you will die in your sins" (John 8:24). Belief in the I AM brings mercy and pardon for sin. Unbelief in Jesus will lead to death. When we sin, and turn to Christ for forgiveness, we can be confident of Jesus' mercy. This brings tremendous psychological and spiritual comfort. We need not walk around with unresolved guilt accusing our conscience. We are objects of God's tender mercy. This should have a profound effect on how we treat one another.

Each morning I pray that God would make me a tender, merciful father to my children. Yet, when I express frustration toward my children, I align myself with the unbelief of the Jews who rejected Jesus. I act as though I have no accountability to the I AM *and* no experience of his mercy toward me in my sins. Only when I'm awake to the reality of God's just and merciful presence do I express his tender mercy toward my children. Oh, that my children would grow up knowing more of God's mercy, and less of my impatient judgment. That I would be a window onto the merciful heart of our heavenly Father. After all, Jesus taught us, "Be merciful, even as your heavenly Father is merciful" (Luke 6:36).

SHOWING MERCY

If we're recipients of divine mercy—not the judgment we deserve—how much more should we show mercy to one another?

Generous mercy. The merciful are slow to judge. You've probably heard the adage "If you're angry, count to ten before responding." This would go a long way in today's outrage-charged society. Consider how mercy would change your response to those you disagree with. When you see a social-media post that rubs you the wrong way, consider counting to ten before judging. Then give it another ten minutes to consider (a) if you've interpreted the post correctly and (b) if it's really worth responding to.

Taking this time to reflect points us toward mercy not judgment. In social-media debates, many readers are triggered by a surface reading of a post and respond immediately, without adequate reflection. So they end up reading their own context into posts. When this happens, the debate that ensues is based on misunderstanding, often resulting in an acrimonious exchange that generates more heat than light. When we don't count to ten before responding, we often make snap judgments.

The merciful are in touch with the fact that they haven't received what they deserve—divine wrath—but in Christ have received more than they deserve—"grace upon grace" (John 1:16). They recognize God's generous mercy towards them and, in turn, show it to others. This way of seeing ourselves—as recipients of undeserving, contra-conditional, radical love—produces an impulse to search ourselves first for fault. The merciful consistently give others the benefit of the doubt.[5]

This is something I have to work at, which is why I admire it so much in others. When my kids drag in the morning, bicker among themselves, and delay our getting out the door on time, I often find myself quick to judge and slow to show mercy. I think, *If you had gotten up when I asked you to . . .*

My wife, on the other hand, is disposed to see the whole picture and show mercy. She gives the benefit of the doubt, such as pointing out that the kids went to bed late, it was a long weekend, or one of them isn't feeling well. She doesn't assume they're ill-intentioned slackers; instead, she recognizes there are always circumstances that make it difficult to be spry and obedient at 6:30 in the morning.

I, however, tend to see through the lens of judgment. I see disobedience, disrespect, and difficulty. I don't take into account that I have been up for an hour, that I've already made the adjustment from sleepyhead to wide awake. Man, I need to quit letting mercy stop at my door!

Sacrificial mercy. Merciful people are also frequently sacrificial. They embrace inconvenience in order to show mercy to others. They don't enjoy piling others up with burdens, but instead consistently relieve the burdens of others. One morning I received a text that read, "You've hurt your mother's feelings. Can you follow up with her?" I was cut to the heart, and I wondered what I'd done. I had called to check on her. For two years she'd been trying to get random atrial fibrillation under control. Her heart rate would spike up to two hundred beats per minute and then slowly die down, leaving her utterly depleted of energy. During the call, I'd made some insensitive suggestions that reflected my ignorance of what she was going through. As we chatted, I began to realize I didn't understand how difficult life had been for her.

Atrial fibrillation can lead to blood clots, a stroke, and even heart failure. So, in addition to being constantly confronted with her mortality, my mother couldn't do the things she loved to do most: work in her flower garden and serve others, especially her children and grandchildren. She simply lacked the energy. I asked her why she hadn't been more honest about how hard life had been. She responded, "I wanted to keep it from you because you have so much responsibility with the kids, the church, and everything. I didn't want to be a burden."

My mom has been relieving burdens so long, it's simply unthinkable for her to impose a burden on others. She has been a burden reliever her whole life. She's constantly serving in the background, cooking, cleaning, writing cards, playing with grandkids, sending thoughtful packages, applying Band-Aids to skinned knees, and most of all, praying. When I feel the need for prayer, she is the first person I call. But in this case she needed prayer, she needed support, she needed her burdens to be relieved. She was so used to giving mercy, she hadn't even thought about receiving mercy from us.

What a striking picture of mercy: to be so concerned with relieving others that you don't think of relief for yourself. Of course, it's important to also receive mercy, but many of us are better at receiving than giving. I want to be more like my mother.

Active mercy. Mercy isn't passive or weak; it is active. We've already seen how intellectually, emotionally, and spiritually active mercy can be, but mercy also gets things done. A truly merciful heart marshals empathy to serve others.

There's a difference between empathy-based action and mercy-based action. Empathy-based action climbs into the sorrows of others and feels them strongly. Empathy can be a wonderful quality, but when we act primarily because of what we feel, we can easily lose our bearings. Empathy is narrowly focused because it's harnessed by an emotion associated with a single person, event, or injustice. Mercy, however, is embedded in our character; this makes it run deeper and spread further.

Several mercy ministries in our church focus on serving marginalized people in low-income apartments. These ministries are built on the conviction that mercy is person-centric not project-based. Therefore much of what we do is focused on knowing people and, out of intimate relationship, discerning how we can best meet practical needs.

Inevitably new volunteers come to these communities eager to *do* something. They may have been moved by a sermon or headline and want to make a difference. But if they don't see visible progress within a few visits, they sometimes ask, "Why haven't we built a new playground?" "When can we build better housing?" They want to *accomplish something*. In part, this is a good thing. They want to make a difference and see physical change. But physical changes uninformed by relationship—and the wisdom that comes from it—can leave people feeling like projects, missing the target entirely. Mercy, however, looks others in the face. It moves us toward those in need, not only because we feel something but also because we want to know someone.

Showing mercy isn't merely getting things done; it's expressing God's kindness to someone with a name.

So you see, the foundations of justice and mercy go way past Plato back to the triune God, etched into his character and self-revelation as the I AM. When we recognize this, we are flattened out and lifted up all at once. We're flattened by God's just gaze at our sinful failure but lifted up by his deep, sacrificial mercy. We are inspired to be generous, sacrificial, and active in mercy—to be slow to judge, quick to give the benefit of the doubt, and eager to act on behalf of others. Merciful people show others what has been and forever will be shown to us in Christ.

OVERCOMING YOUR CHAOS

- ◆ Why does mercy require judgment? How does this challenge your existing view of mercy?

- ◆ Think about a time you felt you were treated unjustly. Why did you feel that way? Did you see it as a transgression against individual freedom, the community, or a cosmic authority?

- ◆ How does God's approach to justice challenge or inspire you? In light of this, what steps can you take to align more with him?

- ◆ Mercy is slow to judge, gives the benefit of the doubt, and is sacrificial. Write down three ways you can express mercy toward others in each of these ways. Commit to practicing them.

- ◆ What is the difference between empathy-based action and mercy-based action? Which do you tend toward? How does Jesus relate to these?

- ◆ How can you consistently keep Jesus in focus as you practice mercy?

Seven

PURITY
IN AN AGE OF
SELF-EXPRESSION

"Blessed are the pure in heart,
for they shall see God."

MATTHEW 5:8

I N THE FILM *FIRST MAN,* astronaut Neil Armstrong is depicted as a sixties strong-and-silent type. The evening before he leaves for the moon, his wife confronts him, insisting she won't be the one to tell their children their father might not come back. Yielding to his wife, Armstrong gathers his family around the kitchen table, where he struggles to find the words and fails to express the empathy and comfort his children long for. It's all he can do to muster a side-hug for his son.

The camera pans out, framing him at the kitchen table, alone, as if to critique the single-minded conformity to his gender role. Throughout the film, Armstrong is frequently seen in the kitchen, but only to draw a glass of water and gaze out the window and up. His wife prepares the meal. Both reflect the gender roles of the sixties.

While the kitchen may be a place for some women, it's not for all. A number of my male friends are great cooks, dazzling their families with culinary delights. My family wasn't graced with such a dad. As a father of two daughters, I love seeing my girls play soccer with the best of them. I secretly gloat when one of them beats my son in a footrace—every single time. But I also delight in my son's unusual sensitivity. Although he's a teenager, he declares multiple times a day, "Coming in for a hug," and wraps his parents up in affection. Affection isn't just for girls, and sports aren't just for boys.

However, there's a difference between gender roles and gender identity. You Be You is an organization that works with educational experts and psychologists to create tools to help students be "the best version of themselves." According to You Be You, the best version of yourself entails creativity to transcend gender stereotypes: "You can be whoever you want to be regardless of gender."[1]

This mission is truly good when liberating men and women from strict cultural notions of gender. But You Be You goes even further, seeing gender not as something you inherit biologically or spiritually but as something you create. You choose your gender because "you" are whatever you want to be. There are no constraints, except one: "to thine own self be true." What drives gender fluidity also drives suspicion toward purity: the right to express ourselves however we want. Sociologist Robert Bellah calls this *expressive individualism*.

INNER PURITY

In expressive individualism, "each person has a unique core of feeling and intuition that should unfold or be expressed if individuality is to be realized."[2] The individual's core feeling is supreme. What matters most is not what others say, or what religion or philosophy says, but *how I feel.* How I date, what I spend my money on, and what I do with my time, family, career, and sexuality are governed by me and no one else. As long as I'm true to myself, to my inner longings and desires, that's what's pure. For the modern self, purity is being consistent with what you feel is good, true, or desirable, not what any outside authority has to say.

Inner purity seeks a new center of authority—the self. In doing so it legitimizes the wants and desires of self, frequently elevating them to the status of needs and rights. Take, for instance, the man who belonged to the National Association to Advance Fat Acceptance and filed a lawsuit against McDonald's because he couldn't fit into any of the restaurant chairs. He reasoned that since 20 percent of Americans are seriously obese, 20 percent of McDonald's chairs should be oversized to accommodate them.[3] The right to express himself eclipsed a sense of his own responsibility and of the potential repercussions of his lawsuit. Instead he elevated his desire to live in dietary unrestraint to such a high degree he was willing to infringe on the rights of a company by seeking to legalize his wants at their cost.

That said, it's very difficult to be fat in our society. For larger customers, eating out can be an awkward experience. Imagine being turned away because seating is inadequate or having to make your party wait as the restaurant rearranges seating to accommodate your body size. So there is room for improvement in how the public views fat people and in how they are treated.[4] But when individuals want legal rights, the sky's the limit. What's to prevent underweight people from filing a lawsuit because McDonald's normal-sized chairs make them feel skinny and self-conscious? And what about the people who have to use a cane to walk but when they sit down, they have nowhere to put the cane? Why not file a lawsuit to get cane holders installed? After all, canes frequently fall down when resting against restaurant walls. Unrestrained desire inevitably reaches a level of absurdity.

Refusing to limit self-expression can also be harmful to society. On May 29, 2015, Ross Ulbricht, a graduate of Penn State, was sentenced to double life imprisonment plus forty years, without the possibility of parole. What was his crime? Starting and running the Silk Road, a black market for the free exchange of goods and services on the dark web. The Silk Road facilitated all kinds of secret transactions, including identity fraud, money laundering, the trafficking of narcotics, assault rifles, poisonous substances, body parts—and even murder.

At one point, the site processed five hundred thousand dollars a week in sales. Ulbricht was making millions. However, his stated reason for starting Silk Road wasn't to get rich but to give people the freedom to buy and sell whatever they want. As a student of libertarian philosophy, he was principally committed to individual freedom and expression, regardless of its impact on society.

When Judge Katherine Forrest passed Ulbricht's double life sentence, she said, "What you did was terribly destructive to our social fabric."[5]

Ulbricht replied, "I'm not a self-centered sociopathic person that was trying to express some inner badness. I do love freedom. I wanted to empower people to be able to make choices in their lives."[6] Contrary to his plea, Ulbricht's love of freedom unleashed inner badness, revealing freedom's need for moral restraint. But he was consistent with his beliefs, reflecting a kind of inner purity. He was true to himself. Unfortunately this came at the expense of the greater good.

EXPRESSIVE INDIVIDUALISM IN THE CHURCH

Just think what would happen if a whole group of people inclined to expressive individualism came together. Someone puts forward a vision for the group; they all agree but then begin to realize their individual passions aren't being adopted by the group. One person is passionate about adoption; another is dedicated to ending human trafficking; yet another is adamant about racial justice. While the passions of each individual are commendable, each wants his or her cause to get more attention.

Another group of people pushes back, saying they have to address a "crisis of eternity" by sharing the gospel more. Some feel their age group is being neglected, while others are lonely and want to experience more community. Meanwhile a number of couples face serious marital issues and can't imagine devoting more emotional resources to other people or causes. They're just holding on for dear life. A few face deep personal issues and require sustained care and counseling, but they feel nobody understands what they're going through. So they decide to look for another community—or church.

Expressive individualism works against the grain of the gospel. The gospel says, "Take up your cross and follow me," but expressive individualism says, "Take up your cause and follow self."

When everyone takes up an individual cause or concern other than Christ, the church turns into a Department of Motor Vehicles. The room is packed with disgruntled people waiting to get their issue serviced. Beady eyes on the counter, they can't wait to get their number called and then get out. Is it any wonder the church struggles to express the gospel to the world or that the world is disinterested in the news we have to share?

Instead of pointing away from ourselves to the supremely satisfying cause of glorifying God and enjoying him forever, we drum our fingers in anxious concern that our agenda isn't being validated. The complicated thing about expressive individualism in the church is that many of the individual concerns are valid. Jesus himself calls us to many of them. The issue, however, is not that our concerns are invalid; it is that they are *ultimate*. They displace the deeper joy of taking up our cross and following Jesus.

What does "take up your cross" mean? In the Roman Empire, criminals carrying a cross to their execution was a public expression of submission to the state. The law had been broken, and walking under a cross signified order that had been restored. When we take up our cross, it's in submission to God's kingdom. We're saying to Jesus, "I submit to and prioritize your rule and order." We renounce the reign of self for the rule of Christ, permitting him to reorder our lives however he sees fit.

The call of the gospel is death to self and life in Christ—every single day. In the succinct words of Dietrich Bonhoeffer, "Every command of Jesus is a call to die."[7] When we break the Savior's commands in favor of pushing our agenda, we betray the most important agenda in the world. Impatience, unkindness, anger, gossip, and despair are all signs that the self has come off the cross—and Christ with it. In its place, our cause weighs heavily.

If we aren't careful, a righteous cause can become an unrighteous bludgeon. We redefine the church based on our individual mission, and we judge those who fail to join it. We reshape pastoral callings, expecting church leaders to function as PR reps, advertising our personal passion. If press is infrequent or inadequate, we fire off an email or post to get them back on track. We redefine the church in the image of our idol.

Although we may be "in church," our identity is "in self." Our mission devolves from preaching nothing but "Christ and him crucified" to adamantly seeking "self and its agenda glorified."

Given the dangers of expressive individualism, should we abandon our causes and concerns? Not at all. We need not sacrifice one command for the sake of others. How then should we move forward?

THREE WAYS TO ADDRESS
OUR AGENDAS

Purity in the age of self requires several things: *repentance, reconciliation,* and *remembrance.* Think of these not as steps but as concentric circles that radiate outward from our core, perhaps like growth rings in a tree.

Repent and believe. In the center is repentance and faith. If we've drifted from following Jesus by taking up an agenda in place of his cross, we must start by confessing our rebellion to him. Where have you thrown off his rule in favor of your agenda?

Begin by identifying broken commands and relationships, or unruly emotions, and trace them to their source in your own heart. What concern or cause has taken the ultimate place in your life? Confess it to Jesus, and ask him to forgive you for your sin. Tell him you have made it a burdensome load and have chosen not to submit to him. Then choose to trust and to submit to his reign. Remember, his burden is light and his yoke is easy. Ask him to help you trust him with your issue, including when it is met, how it is met, and the progress made.

Reconcile relationships. Second, look to reconcile any relationships that have been strained or broken as a result of your agenda. Stay inside the circles of reconciliation and repentance; don't look for where others have failed you. Instead look to reconcile your own failures. You can't change others, but humble repentance often breeds change in those around us. Magnify your common hope and identity in Jesus.

Remember the gospel. Third, look for ways you can make progress with your concern or cause while remembering the gospel. What steps can you take to increase community, grow in evangelism, or promote justice while remembering this Beatitude: "Blessed are the merciful, for they shall receive mercy" (Matthew 5:7). Make progress by remembering how much mercy God has shown you in your years of ignorance of and indifference to your particular issue. As you pursue justice, remember how Jesus stood in your place to show you mercy. As you seek community, recall how he suffered to give you a place in his family. As you evangelize, remind yourself of God's patience with you in responding to his good news. Try to avoid judging others by remembering mercy and giving others the benefit of the doubt. And recognize that not everyone has your calling.

Living within these circles of repentance, reconciliation, and remembrance, we are likely to win others to our cause. But our ultimate goal must remain: taking up our cross and following Jesus *together*. This glorifies God over self and attracts others to our Savior's sage authority.

Pure devotion to self dispenses with community, self-sacrifice, and the greater good. Unlimited expression of individual desire is untenable. If everyone got their way, society would devolve into chaos and relationships into ruin. Individual expression must be held in check by something. What is the right standard to restrain expressive individualism? Perhaps the moral order of the sixties was on to something when it emphasized "doing the right thing."

OUTER PURITY

Another way to determine what's pure is to focus not on inner feelings but on outward action. It's what you *do* when nobody's looking that counts. The key is steady moral character regardless of how you feel.

This approach to life produced the Greatest Generation, a generation of people who got America through the Great Depression and World War II, securing the freedom and material prosperity we enjoy today. I wonder how my generation or the iGeneration would fare in such difficult circumstances.

The Greatest Generation was governed by a moral principle very different from the commitment to individual freedom. They were dutifully bound to doing the right thing. This unflappable commitment to duty and to society produced Neil Armstrong who, when stepping onto the moon, said, "One small step for man, one giant leap for mankind."

What would someone committed to self-expression say when accomplishing such a feat? "One giant leap by me"—then snap a selfie and post it on Instagram? Expressive individualism uses society to serve self, but the Greatest Generation used self to serve society.

Doing the right thing for the wrong reason. Benjamin Franklin, a quintessential American who embodied an ethic like that of the Greatest Generation, also focused on outward action. He founded the University of Pennsylvania and Philadelphia's first fire department, invented the lightning rod and bifocals, and became a prominent abolitionist and the first Postmaster General, to name just a few of his accomplishments. He attributed his great success to living according to "a little book" that described thirteen Christian virtues.

However, Franklin reshaped some of these classical virtues to reflect a utilitarian ethic. In particular, he described "chastity" (or purity) as never injuring your own reputation. Notice that he didn't emphasize feelings, wants, or intention but action and reputation. This emphasis on outward action surfaces in some expressions of Christianity: "Don't drink, dance, or chew, or go with those who do." Read your Bible, go to church, and pray.

However, action to preserve a reputation quickly devolves into cold moralism. Jumping through moralistic hoops or doing things just because others say to rings hollow. Alternatively Christians may focus on having "pure doctrine," a sort of intellectual or theological purity that sets them above others, regardless of their languishing affection for Christ or love for others. Emphasis on outer action is what led Jesus to call the Pharisees "whitewashed tombs," clean on the outside, dead on the inside (Matthew 23:27).

For all his accomplishments and accolades, Franklin fell short in a few areas. His emphasis on getting things done came at the expense of neglecting others. He was notoriously absent from home, spending years abroad in London and Paris, apart from his family. In one stretch, he was gone from his wife and children for ten years, while his wife had two strokes. He frequently wrote to her, promising to return home soon, but failed to do so. As an absent father, his relationship with his eldest son grew tense, eventually leading to estrangement.

What was Franklin doing all those years? In addition to lobbying to curb the proprietary powers of the Penn family and representing the interests of the colonies, he was indulging his libido. He was known to frequent brothels and had quite a few mistresses, one of whom bore him a son named William. Franklin recorded some of his exploits in his autobiography and letters, some of which were not published until much later. One infamous letter, dubbed "Advice to a Friend on Choosing a Mistress," includes counsel in how to channel sexual urges and pick out a mistress. All this from a man who promoted a life of morality through his thirteen virtues.

But does sexual purity really matter? Should we have to conform to sexual norms? According to the General Social Survey, in 1973 about 70 percent of respondents described adulterous sex as "always wrong." In 2016, this percentage was actually higher—about 76 percent.[8]

Curbing sexual desire can be very good for society. When people restrain their lust, it creates less demand for things like prostitution and sex trafficking. And sexual faithfulness can contribute to family cohesiveness. Just think how different Franklin's family would have been if he had been faithful to his wife.

However, outer purity is not enough. Couples who stay together through acrimony and lovelessness may preserve the family unit but end up dismantling it from the inside out. If inner desires go unchecked, outer actions eventually ring hollow. Sexual ethics matter, but doing the right thing for the wrong reason can be just as destructive as doing the wrong thing.

Of course, actions matter even if our motivations aren't noble. Say you're serving with a group at a local homeless shelter. A couple hundred homeless men and women line up to get a hot meal and a warm smile from caring people. Mary, one of the girls on your team, is chatting with one of the hungry homeless guys. All of a sudden she pulls out her phone to take a selfie with the man. Then she holds up the line while posting to Instagram, "Love serving the needy in our city!" Afterward she gets right back to work, serving with a smile. Is it possible Mary was motivated by vanity or self-righteousness as she served the poor? Yes. Does that render her service useless? No. Taking time out of her busy schedule to serve the marginalized of her city is a good thing. But is it a virtuous thing? Was it pure? Probably not.

Recalling Aristotle, virtue is when inner motivation and outer action come into alignment as a relatively fixed part of our character. One-off or occasional service with the goal of looking good on social media or to fluff the résumé isn't virtuous, but we would be foolish to say that those actions have no value. A couple hundred hungry people were served with a smile.

While actions do matter, our inner motivations can simultaneously be impure. We can "do the right thing" for the wrong reasons—the applause of others, affirmation on social media, or good standing in society. Virtue requires both purity of motivation and action. Although Ulbricht was true to himself, he needed moral correction. While Franklin attributed his success to his behavior, he lacked an inner purity to set him straight. How do we bring motivation and action together to achieve true purity? Jesus' solution is purity of the heart.

BEING PURE IN HEART

When Jesus said, "Blessed are the pure in heart," what did he mean? His vision of purity is drawn from Psalm 24, which describes an ancient mountain, luxuriant and green, with a city built right into it. All who live there have their own vine and fig tree (Micah 4:4; Zechariah 3:10). Food and drink are in abundant supply. The economy is good, and people lack for nothing. Men, women, and children *flourish*.

At the top of the mountain is a beauty so pure it puts Athena in its shadow. But the only way to gain access to the mountain, to put down roots in the city, is to climb to the top and stand before Pure Beauty and pass her test. She has to look you in the eye, down into your soul, and see total purity. To admit anyone who isn't innocent would ruin their way of life. If she sees purity, you receive her blessing and get to live on the mountain forever. If she doesn't, you're banished from the mountain.

So how do we pass the test? The psalmist put it like this: "Who shall ascend the hill of the LORD? And who shall stand in his holy place? He who has clean hands and a pure heart, who does not lift up his soul to what is false and does not swear deceitfully. He will receive blessing from the LORD" (24:3-5). Jesus' promised blessing is for those who have clean hands *and* a pure heart. Good actions are not enough. Nor is being true to yourself. Nothing less than inner and outer purity is required.

For the soul to flourish, it must be lifted up in truth, not deceit. But who among us has this kind of integrity? Can we not identify with Ulbricht's naive devotion to his own heart? How many times a day do we hold court in our heads, only to acquit ourselves of wrongdoing because "our heart was in the right place"? Or commit Franklin's folly, praising ourselves for doing the right thing though we didn't want to? Even if we are true to our inner purity, it will result in an outer impurity. And if we dedicate ourselves to outer purity, a self-righteous inner purity is sure to emerge. Yet our culture encourages this broken and bifurcated approach to virtue.

In the movie *Shazam*, an ancient, dying wizard seeks someone who is "pure of heart" to take his place. His successor will possess great power, which is to be used to keep seven deadly demons at bay, each representing one of the seven deadly sins. After an exhaustive search through time, the wizard eventually finds Billy Batson, a boy who is pure of heart.

When Billy receives his powers, he turns into a buff adult version of himself. He possesses superspeed, superstrength, and the ability to fly and to cast lightning from his fingers. At first he uses his power for good, but eventually his immaturity gets the best of him. He steals candy and beer, entertains for money, neglects people in need, and transports himself to a gentlemen's club more than once.

Apparently the writer and director saw no conflict between Billy's "pure heart" and his self-absorbed lust. He just needed some shaping up. As the film's tagline states, "We all have a superhero inside us, it just takes a bit of magic to bring it out."

Wrong. We all have a superego inside us. We possess divided hearts. In the words of Russian novelist and political activist Aleksandr Solzhenitsyn, "If only there were evil people somewhere insidiously committing evil deeds, and it were necessary only to separate them from the rest of us and destroy them. But the line dividing good and evil cuts through the heart of every human being."[9] Magic is not enough to purify the human heart.

A grand fissure exists between the outer and the inner life that only the love of God can heal. And for that healing to occur, we must admit our lack of integrity. In the words of Martyn Lloyd-Jones, "the only way to have a pure heart is to realize you have an impure heart."[10] We must admit to God and to ourselves that we lift our souls to another, to that which is false and not true. Only then can we face the test honestly. This, of course, guarantees failure. With unclean hands and an impure heart, how can anyone pass the test and gain entrance to the mountain? We need a cure so powerful it heals us inside and out.

As the story unfolds, something unexpected happens. Pure Beauty, the king of Glory, comes down the mountain and enters our divided world. He lives among us, escapes every temptation, and lives a sinless life among sinful people. He doesn't lift his soul to another, nor does he keep his secrets to himself. He generously teaches the way to live a blessed life and demonstrates its beauty. But as it turns out, teaching and serving are not enough.

His pure teachings inspire and condemn but cannot heal the divided heart. Healing can occur only from the inside out. So before he leaves, he draws human impurity to himself like a magnet, knowing the sheer force of it will crush him. In giving his life, he absorbs our sin. In taking his life back up, through glorious resurrection, he secures our spotless status. He offers his purity in exchange for our impurity.

All that's required is to lift our soul to Pure Beauty and say, "Wash me, make me clean. Not only my hands, but my heart, my all." Christ welcomes the divided heart, cleanses sullied motives, and unites us with his undying love. This stroke of ineffable mercy unites not only heart and hands but also our soul to him. We are made one with Pure Beauty, so that when he looks upon us, he sees a shimmering reflection of his own glory: inner and outer beauty. What we lack, he imparts. Where we're divided, he unites. Purity, it turns out, is not accomplished by us but by him.

This can sound both wonderful and bogus. I stand before Pure Beauty with his purity imparted to me? With my soul lifted to him, I become one with him and pass the test? Why, then, does my heart still wander and do my hands still get dirty?

How do we keep from reverting to the old dualism, privileging outer or inner purity?

By practicing the rest of the Beatitude: *seeing God.*

SEEING GOD

We see God through Scripture and nature. These two lenses bring God into focus, allowing us to begin to make out his features, character, and beauty. Scripture is the first lens because it is crystal clear. The second half of Psalm 19 makes this clear: "The law of the LORD is perfect, / reviving the soul" (v.7). Scripture doesn't just give us information about God; it mediates the presence of God. Its perfection is *his* perfection. That's why it revives the heart. Our soul is moved as we read, not primarily because Scripture is reliable but because it is relational. The word of God is the perfect personal speech of God *to us.*

Over and over again the Scriptures record, "Thus said the Lord" or "The word of the Lord came to. . . ." The Bible claims to be the speech of God. When you hear someone's voice in another room, you can tell who it is without even seeing her. Why? Because her speech is unique; it reveals her and not somebody else. Similarly God's words are uniquely personal; they reveal *him.* The Bible is God speaking in space and time—to us.

God also speaks through *nature.*

The heavens declare the glory of God,
>   and the sky above proclaims his handiwork.
Day to day pours out speech,
>   and night to night reveals knowledge.
There is no speech, nor are there words,
>   whose voice is not heard. (Psalm 19:1-3)

According to the first half of Psalm 19, God doesn't just speak; he declares, proclaims, and pours out his speech through creation. What is he saying? Nature announces his glory, which is the radiant sum total of his perfect attributes.

When I lingered at the edge of the Grand Canyon, taking in the sprawling striated rock a mile deep and eighteen miles wide, nature put me in touch with God's immensity. Theologian Louis Berkhof describes God's immensity as "that perfection of the Divine Being that transcends all spatial limitations."[11] Unfortunately this doctrine is infrequently taught or discussed, and yet it is one of the most urgent in the Age of the Big Me.

Purifying vision. Taking in God's immensity humbles the ego and lifts the soul. True greatness puts us in our place, enabling us to appreciate the beauty of God's character and grace. When I go for a walk in the Ladybird Wildflower Center, following the meandering paths of crushed rock that wind through the Texas hill country, I often pause to observe the dragon-mouthed bluebonnets and red trumpets of cedar sage. There I'm moved by God's creativity and love. But without God's self-revelation in Scripture, I wouldn't know to trace these to the triune God. The two lenses of Scripture and nature work together to bring God into focus, enabling us to see more of him.

But how do these glimpses of God make us pure? When people are dating, we often say, "He is seeing her." By *see* do we mean an occasional stare? No, we mean two people have taken such an interest in one another, they cut out other things to spend time together. But "seeing one another" also means more. It means seeing one another even when they don't *see* one another. How so? We take images of people we want to see with us—sometimes literally—so that we can see them. When we miss them, we reflect on a meaningful time with them or pull out a phone and flip through our photos. Seeing God works in a similar way. It doesn't require sitting in nature or meditation all day long. Instead we can take a snapshot of his character or his words, and pull it back out throughout the day.

In a lull between activities, instead of burying myself in my Twitter feed, I sometimes recall an image from my morning devotions and linger over it. I pull out the photo and reflect on the most beautiful being in the universe. This moves me away from seeking attention on social media to enjoying God's attention. It's much more satisfying, and it purifies narcissistic tendencies. If I'm challenged by a task at work, I recall God's immensity seen in the Grand Canyon or the Psalms to find encouragement to keep going. I also pull out a snapshot when I realize I've failed in some way. If I'm tempted to wallow in guilt, I recall Jesus clothed in bright linen, draping me in robes of white (Daniel 7:9; Revelation 1:13; 3:4; 4:4). This scriptural memory purifies my inclination to wallow in poor little me. It also redirects me to my gracious Savior. By recalling images of God throughout the day, we are purified to look more like him and less like the sinful version of ourselves.

One day, snapshots will no longer be necessary. The apostle John wrote, "We know that when he appears we shall be like him, because we shall see him as he is" (1 John 3:2). Beholding God in his perfect glory triggers a promised transformative moment: *we will be like him.* No more grappling with inner and outer purity. We will be whole, fully integrated by a single glance, never again to struggle with impure motives or actions. We will flourish on the mountain forever! Until then, John reminds us the future *must* impact the present: "And everyone who thus hopes in him purifies himself as he is pure" (1 John 3:3). We can see God now and be pure in heart.

OVERCOMING YOUR CHAOS

- ◆ Think of instances in which you've counseled yourself or others toward inner purity. Why is this counsel inadequate? How can you restate this counsel?
- ◆ Why does expressive individualism hurt the church? How have you insisted on your own way at the expense of your community or church? Take time to confess and repent of this sin and to enjoy God's grace.
- ◆ What are the strengths and weaknesses of outer purity? Which strengths do you need to embrace better?
- ◆ Read Psalm 24. How does this inspire purity? What verses can you memorize to help you practice purity?
- ◆ How does Jesus heal the fissure between inner and outer purity?
- ◆ What are specific ways you can improve your ability to see God each day? Commit to one this week.

Eight

PEACEMAKING IN AN AGE OF OUTRAGE

*"Blessed are the peacemakers, for
they shall be called sons of God."*

MATTHEW 5:9

J ULIA THOUGHT IT WOULD BE A GOOD idea to
volunteer in her son's kindergarten classroom during the
Christmas holidays. When she got to school, she was assigned
to the musical chairs station. Realizing no one had been asked
to play music, she pulled out her phone to find a song. Since
the theme of the week was reindeers, she decided to play
"Rudolph the Red-Nosed Reindeer." The kids sang and
scrambled for seats.

Afterward a mom approached Julia and told her the song
wasn't appropriate. A second mother chimed in, saying, "Yeah,
we want to be really inclusive." Puzzled, Julia shared her

experience with a friend. She discovered that "Rudolph the Red-Nosed Reindeer" had become the subject of an online debate over its bullying content. Huffington Post had tweeted a clip from the Christmas classic, suggesting it was "seriously problematic." The post spawned more than eight thousand responses on Twitter, with outrage spilling onto other platforms and into real-life classrooms. The outrage dampened Christmas spirits and obscured the redemptive ending of the song: all the other reindeer end up loving Rudolph, and he gets to guide Santa's sleigh.

A CULTURE OF OUTRAGE

Despite the silliness of some outrage, social media indignation can be *good*. In December 2013, Justine Sacco, communications director for InterActiveCorp, posted the following message on Twitter: "Going to Africa. Hope I don't get AIDS. Just kidding. I'm white!" She was mobbed online by people justly excoriating her for her racist comment. As it turns out, Sacco had a history of racist and morally unsavory tweets, which seems ironic for a communications director.

In a unique twist, Sacco was on an international flight while the outrage swelled. During her flight, the hashtag #hasjustine-landedyet was created, and people were calling for her termination. Shortly after she landed, she was fired, and she issued a public apology. Social media outrage had generated a helpful correction.

Outraged comments can also create an offense *greater* than the original infraction. In response, people expressed a desire for Sacco to get AIDS, be raped, and even murdered. Reflecting on the disproportionate outrage, *New York Times* writer Teddy Wayne wrote, "Though we are quick to condemn callousness and prejudice as a form of bullying, we less readily interrogate our own participation, even as bystanders, in the widespread attack of a single person, which is a classic example of bullying."[1] While we may be quick to call out bullying in a Christmas classic, we're slower to recognize our own online bullying. It's tempting to pile on negativity, swear words, and hate when someone says something that opposes our values or beliefs. And if we believe self-expression is our greatest right, we'll rarely exercise restraint.

In fact, anger is the emotion most easily spread across social media.

One study shows that those who succumb to outrage tend to be angrier people who fail to address their anger in healthy ways. This suggests an immoral root behind outrage. Wayne proposes self-righteousness: "By throwing 140-character stones from our Google Glass houses, we preserve our belief (or delusion) that we are morally superior to those who have offended us."[2] Indeed, digital stone throwing is easy; we don't even have to wind up.

Self-righteous belief and delusion were on display when a partial video of Covington Catholic High School student Nick Sandmann encountering a Native American man, Nathan Phillips, went viral. The video appeared to be an antagonistic standoff between white Trump supporters and indigenous rally members, when in fact it was something quite different. But it was too late, as the video inspired a storm of angry insults and misinformed hot takes, the ensuing polarization whipped up in an online frenzy. Within two days of the encounter, thousands of people signed an online petition to remove the principal of Covington. The student was vilified as all that is wrong with America, and the Native American was praised for his professional activism.

As it turns out, a group of Hebrew Israelites were taunting both the Native Americans and the Catholic high school students. Since the crowd of students was larger than the Hebrew Israelites group, Nathan Phillips drummed his way into the group of boys in order to pray and promote peace. Phillips inadvertently ended up facing Sandmann. Unaware of Phillips intentions, Sandmann issued a smile, interpreted online as a smirk. Sandmann later said, "I wanted [Phillips] to know that I was not going to become angry, intimidated or be provoked into a larger confrontation."[3] Once the context of the video came out, some retracted their social media posts and apologized. Others dug in.

It is tempting to read online posts from a high horse instead of a humble heart. When we look down on those who disagree with us, it's easy to justify moral ultimatums, broad generalizations, and cynical remarks. Alternatively it's easy to make hot takes as we pander for approval from the online masses. Since many platforms identify who we are, our responses are traced back to us, giving us favor with those we want to impress. I'm often tempted to respond to an online issue, not merely because I agree or disagree, but also to communicate my care about the issue. A private response, however, such as studying the issue further, praying for those affected, or having a constructive conversation with a friend is often much more fruitful. Anonymity, of course, doesn't scratch the self-righteous itch.

Platforms that have limited character-number responses play to anger, disallowing the space and time required to think through and winsomely respond to an issue. While internet outrage can accomplish good things, very often it's less than constructive. It's also less likely to promote peace. In the words of Nelson Mandela, "When we dehumanize and demonize our opponents, we abandon the possibility of peacefully resolving our differences, and seek to justify violence against them."[4] When we exaggerate differences, we distort people instead of respecting them. How can we broker peace when our egos are so fragile and moral discernment is so weak?

A CULTURE OF FRAGILITY

While some of us are tempted to outrage, others of us are drawn into self-protection. In a timely study of trends in American universities, Greg Lukianoff and Jonathan Haidt pointed out that students have been increasingly drawn into what they describe as *safetyism*—a culture or belief system in which safety is a sacred value.[5] Starting in 2013, a majority of university students began to embrace the idea they should not be exposed to "offensive" ideas. As a result, universities experienced a spike in the disinvitation of public speakers to campus, not because students disagreed with their ideas but because they found them "harmful." Haidt and Lukianoff point to this collegiate sacralizing of safety as a symptom of a wider cultural phenomenon—a culture of fragility.

The authors of *The Coddling of the American Mind* tell the story of Olivia, a Latina student at Claremont McKenna College, who published an essay in a student publication about her feelings of marginalization and exclusion.[6] Observing a deficit of Latinos among the professional staff and a better representation of them among blue-collar staff, Olivia expressed that she felt as though she'd been admitted to fill a racial quota. She felt she didn't fit in an institutional culture "primarily grounded in western, white, cisheteronormative upper-middle class values."[7] Two days after receiving an email of the essay from Olivia, Mary Spellman, the dean of students, sent her this email response:

Olivia—

Thank you for writing and sharing this article with me. We have a lot to do as a college and community. Would you be willing to talk with me sometime about these issues? They are important to me and the [dean of students] staff and we are working on how we can better serve students, especially those who don't fit our CMC mold.

I would love to talk to you more.

Best,

Dean Spellman

Olivia responded by posting Spellman's email on her Facebook page with the comment, "I just don't fit that wonderful CMC mold! Feel free to share." A campus protest erupted: marches, demonstrations, and hunger strikes, accompanied by demands for Spellman to resign. Spellman apologized for wording the email poorly but stood by her intention to affirm the feelings in the article and provide support. The students refused her apology, with one woman berating Spellman until she broke down in tears. While the university did not fire

Spellman, it failed to express public support of her. With escalating anger, social media outrage, and national news coverage, Spellman resigned.

Why did this happen? While there are layers to any conflict, Haidt and Lukianoff suggest that if Olivia had responded charitably, interpreting Spellman's email in its best possible light, things could have been resolved much more peacefully. Instead Olivia took a word out of context, did not respond to Spellman directly, published her misinterpretation online, and refused to accept a heartfelt apology. Olivia and Spellman were reduced to categories: victim and oppressor.

While there are real victims and oppressors, we should be cautious about seeing ourselves and others through these categories. Reducing people to these types leads to tribalism, an us-versus-them mentality in which neither the "victim" nor the "oppressor" is worthy of dignity or love.[8]

Tribalism reinforces a culture of fragility and outrage. In Spellman's case, her own institution was so fragile and afraid of blowback, it refused to offer her public support. Olivia played to outrage, refusing to accept the humble offer made by Spellman, and she chose to misconstrue information online. But think what could have happened at Claremont McKenna College if the administration had been braver and the student been more charitable? What if civil, face-to-face engagement had occurred instead, with the aim of mutual understanding, necessary institutional reform, and peaceful resolution? What if we weren't so fragile?

In a culture of fragility, one of the "great untruths" embraced is "What doesn't kill you makes you weaker." Ideas, beliefs, and views that ruffle feathers or challenge one's beliefs are transmuted into something harmful. And yet the university was founded with the vision of creating a space for liberal education where young minds engage in the free exchange of ideas.

Hanna Holborn Gray, former president of the University of Chicago, notes: "Education should not be intended to make people comfortable; it is meant to make them think."[9] However, as Haidt and Lukianoff pointed out, emotion—not reason—has taken the place of privilege in moral reasoning. This, they say, is the second great untruth: "Always trust your feelings." When personal feelings become the primary arbiter of what's true, mass outrage and an absence of interpersonal peace are inevitable.

EMBRACING ADVERSITY

When we embrace a culture of fragility, we surrender the character-building value of adversity. Adversity is the crucible of character. In it we're forced to reckon with ourselves. As we noted in chapter two, mourning is meant to force us below the surface of everyday life to discover the kind of people we truly are. However, if adversity is recast from tutor to enemy, we settle for an idealized version of ourselves. If we refuse to learn and retreat from the fight, we will believe our own best press, refusing to admit realities that could make us better people.

Jesus calls us to be peacemakers, which assumes the presence of conflict. He knew tension in relationships is God's appointed grace for moral and spiritual change. Therefore the solution to outrage is not to retreat to the enclave of victim, where we console ourselves with the many wrongs done to us. That fragile world is as dangerous as it is inaccurate. Nor do we stand our ground inflexibly, spewing hot takes, unwilling to enter into true reflection and dialog. Rather, the path forward is to embrace adversity with meekness, humbly seeking change and peace.

It was through Rudolph the Red-Nosed Reindeer's adversity of being bullied and rejected that he opened up to an acceptance and love outside his peer group. As he looked to Santa's favor, he embraced a new vocation and ended up "going down in history."

While our struggles may not put us in the history books, our caring Father observes every agony. And through adversity we come to a deeper knowledge of his love. In fact, enjoying a love from outside our own peer groups, online or otherwise, enables us to avoid the trap of self-righteous outrage or self-consoling fragility.

The two cultures of outrage and fragility represent two potential responses in conflict. Outrage culture fosters a rapid, self-righteous response; the culture of fragility encourages withdrawal and avoidance. Both forgo the more arduous and rewarding path of peacemaking.

WHAT IS PEACE?

If these two cultures work against peacemaking, what should peacemaking actually look like? How do we overcome our tendencies to avoid conflict or escalate it? To answer these questions, we first need to grasp the meaning of *peace*. We often think of peace in remedial terms: the absence of conflict, no tension in relationships, or the cessation of war. While remedying negative things is helpful, it doesn't adequately produce the kind of peace Jesus has in mind or the peace we really long for. His peace is meant to be constructive, increasing harmony, wholeness, and flourishing.

In 1994, eight hundred thousand Tutsis were slaughtered and a million children orphaned in Rwanda. This brutal genocide tore the country apart, devastating its social fabric, economy, and national psyche. And yet there is peace today. No more war, no more ethnic violence. Discriminatory ethnic cards have been banned, and an ambitious program of national unity has been implemented.

For many, however, this peace is incomplete. As the twenty-year anniversary of the conflict approached, journalist Chris McGreal visited the country to interview Tutsi survivors.[10] He discovered underlying unrest as those survivors described walking the streets of Rwanda and looking into the eyes of their family's killers. Although hundreds of thousands of accused murderers were locked up in prison, most had not faced trial. In an effort to restore the peace, the government took up a program to dispense with tribal names, an understandable though questionable effort to move national unity forward.

Lucie, a Tutsi survivor comments, "They want to forget the genocide. We want to remember." Despite commendable improvements, the progress of peace came without the resolution of justice. So the peace achieved was shallow. The entire country yearned for something deeper.

The vision of shalom. Jesus' vision of peacemaking is deeper and broader than superficial peace. It is *shalom*. Shalom is wholeness, integrity, restoration. It's remedial and restorative, the absence of conflict and the presence of wholeness. Calvin Theological Seminary's President Cornelius Plantinga describes shalom as "the webbing together of God, humans and all creation in justice, fulfillment, and delight."[11] This sweeping vision of wholeness resonates with human longing. It's what Lucie craved. It is what the bullied and the bully need.

Shalom is what's missing when social media outrage erupts and fragile hearts withdraw. Without shalom, relationships and countries plunge into darkness. At the heart of this darkness is an unraveling of shalom manifested in sin. Sin strikes out on its own against God's goodness, disrupts relationships, and tears away at the wholeness of society. God hates sin because it spoils his shalom. Sin unfits the world and sends it reeling into discord, disputes, deviance, and war. Jesus wants the opposite for his creation, Rwanda, our communities, you, and me. So how do we get shalom?

Trappist monk and theologian Thomas Merton is believed to have said, "We are not at peace with others because we are not at peace with ourselves, and we are not at peace with ourselves because we are not at peace with God." Without first being reconciled to God, we lack the capacity and perseverance to be peacemaking people. We can't extend what we do not have. Without reconciliation to God, all other attempts to restore peace are necessarily flawed and temporal. If sin results in the unwebbing of God, humans, and all creation in justice, fulfillment, and delight, it follows we need the "God of peace" to put it all back together.

As it turns out, "God of peace" is a moniker for the Lord. The apostle Paul frequently comforted churches with a reminder that this is their God: "May the God of peace be with you all. Amen"

(Romans 15:33; see also 1 Corinthians 14:33; Philippians 4:9; 1 Thessalonians 5:23; Hebrews 13:20).

Securing shalom. So how does the God of peace reestablish shalom? According to the Christ hymn in Colossians 1, peace is established "by the blood of his cross" (v. 20). This stunning hymn describes Jesus securing peace by means of his creative and reconciling power. Holding all things together, he is able to reconcile *to himself* all things, whether on earth or in heaven, making peace by his blood. The costly requirement was not lost on him as he proclaimed over the mass of those gathered around him, "Blessed are the peacemakers." Jesus saw a single path to make this Beatitude a reality, a path that led straight to his own crucifixion. He knew that for people to become peacemakers, they would first have to become "sons of God."

But why does shalom require blood? The solution can seem arcane. If we need to resolve a dispute today, we hire a mediator, perhaps a lawyer; but no one needs to spill blood. So why the blood? We are not dealing with an ordinary human-to-human conflict. This conflict is between humanity and the Divine. As a result, the grievance is much, much greater. It is one thing to reconcile a bitter dispute in a broken marriage but quite another to reconcile grand treason against the sovereign Creator and Sustainer of all things.

All of us have contributed to the disruption of shalom, something a lawyer cannot fix. Our sin is against an infinite God, so we are deserving of an infinite punishment. Therefore, in order to reconcile the relationship between humanity and God, we need more than a finite lawyer. We need someone human enough to bear our punishment but infinite enough to endure it. We need a God-man. The Christ hymn reminds us that the fullness of deity dwells in Jesus, who with shortness of breath gasped, "It is finished." Nothing less than Jesus crucified gets humanity reconciled to God. Jesus humbly and lovingly reconciles us to *himself* by the blood of his cross, welcoming us into the home of his shalom.

The difference of shalom. How, then, does Christ-secured shalom make a difference in interpersonal conflict? When Rick Warren, evangelical pastor and author, was invited to help Rwanda become a "purpose-driven" country, he developed a PEACE plan to help the country recover. The plan sought to establish peace through planting churches, equipping leaders, assisting the poor, caring for the sick, and educating the next generation. But Warren quickly realized they couldn't make progress in economic rebuilding and microenterprise until they first addressed the relational discord in the country.

With Warren's help, the Rwandan government recognized they needed more than an "enforced peace." As a result, they began to hold *gacaca*, a traditional form of justice that was reconfigured to serve as a mix of trial, truth-telling, and reconciliation. Since preachers placed a heavy emphasis on biblical notions of confession and forgiveness, the government looked to local churches for support. Tharcisse Karugarama, Rwanda's justice minister, commented, "All the talk of heaven and hell and redemption helped to start people talking."[12]

Once the specific sins of murder and dismemberment were confessed in public to family members, the offended were able to look the killers in the face and extend forgiveness. Reconciliation began to take place. Although this process was incredibly painful, deeper peace was forged through the confession of sin, forgiveness, and reconciliation uniquely available in Jesus. If the Rwandans can do it, we can do it.

PEACE WITH ONE ANOTHER

When we look our offended party in the face and confess our sin, the God of peace draws from his infinite love to smile at us and say, "I forgive you for slaughtering my Son." With this unmatched, unlimited peacemaking power at our disposal, Christians should be among the very best at making peace with one another. Yet when I consider my own attempts to make peace, mentally scrolling through my contacts, I find it difficult to identify the peacemakers. What makes peace so challenging to cultivate?

Certainly the cultures of outrage and fragility are a factor, but within those cultures lurks a general predisposition to relationships. Those of us who slip into the culture of fragility tend to regard the relationship over the person. Because we're unwilling to risk loss of relationship, we often refrain from telling others the truth. *We want to be liked* more than we want peace. As a result, we often choose to empathize with others or turn a blind eye to the real issue.

Say you have a friend who is a known gossip. You've heard her tear down others repeatedly. Eventually word gets back to you that she has been gossiping about some of your financial decisions. You decide to confront her about this destructive pattern. When you sit down together, instead of being honest about the pattern you see in her life, you glaze over her character flaw, simply telling her that she hurt your feelings. She responds by getting defensive, saying it wasn't really gossip and that she didn't mean anything by it. Afraid of how she might respond if you point out other instances of gossip, you decide to back off. You walk away glad the relationship is intact but disappointed she didn't own her offense. You wonder if she might do it again. You settle for cheap peace. What we need is real peace.

Those of us who succumb to the culture of outrage tend to *want to be right more than we want peace*. We value our perspective over the person. Because we believe our perspective is right, we speak to others (in person or online) without humility. If we're unwilling to entertain the idea that we may be wrong or that there may be more to the issue than we comprehend, we lack the meekness peacemaking requires. We settle for an imposed victory, with our occupying forces "maintaining the peace."

Say someone in your church posts something online you find offensive. You're so disturbed by it, you can't get it out of your head; it's all you can think about for five minutes. So you fire back a snarky response in front of everyone. Clearly she's in the wrong, and it's up to you to correct her. Her response isn't satisfying; she clearly doesn't get it. You're like a coiled spring. As you mull over her comment, you break down her position in your mind. Angrily you jump off social media. The next time you see this person at church, things are awkward. You can think only about how wrong she was. There's no peace between you, but at least you let her know where you stand.

How would a peacemaker respond in these situations? A peacemaker does not regard the relationship over the person, valuing approval over peace. Nor does a peacemaker value their perspective over the person, settling for being right. Instead, a peacemaker honors others by humbly approaching them to reconcile. When we enter a conflict with reconciliation and peace as our primary goal, it changes our disposition and reframes our expectations. However, if we see conflict as an opportunity either to prove we're right or to experience loss, reconciliation will be almost impossible. A peacemaker chooses to approach tension in relationships as God's appointed grace for mutual change.

As we saw with Joseph, God sovereignly intends good for us in every evil. His design is to work all things, including conflict and crisis, for good. How? By conforming us to the image of his Son (Romans 8:29). Hope enters the picture when we choose to see conflict the way God does. If we don't begin to embrace this disposition before conflict, it will be extremely difficult to have it when the moment of conflict arises. But if we embrace this approach to relationships and repeatedly decide to do so, it will put us on the path to peace and Christlike character.

PRACTICES OF A PEACEMAKER

What does all of this look like practically? Let's consider three practices and apply each one to the conflicts already mentioned.

First, pray. Include God in your conflict at the outset by taking your offense to him. Tell him how it makes you feel and what you're struggling to believe. Be honest with him. Remember, this situation is appointed by God to draw you closer to him. As you pray, take up the posture of many of the psalms, "Search me, O God" (Psalm 77:6; 139:23). Draw a circle around yourself and ask God to reveal any sin inside the circle. Repent and receive his forgiveness. Enjoy God's grace.

Second, evaluate. Evaluate the offense to determine whether it is a matter to overlook or to confront. Christians are repeatedly called to overlook offenses, for "love covers a multitude of sins" (1 Peter 4:8; see also Proverbs 10:12; 19:11). A multitude is *a lot.* We should frequently overlook hurts and offenses out of love for others. If we find out someone has gossiped about us, but we don't really know him or it is a one-off offense, the path of peace would be to overlook it. We should overlook sins done to us because God overlooks many of our sins done to him. In fact, God is so merciful he doesn't confront us with every offense. He only occasionally reveals sin to us, allowing us to enjoy his mercy. Surely we should extend this same kindness to others!

If we're called to overlook an offense, we can be at peace with others without going any further in the process. If God does call us to overlook a wrong, then it will be important to continue overlooking the wrong whenever it pops up in our memory. We must refuse the temptation to pull it out and look at it later; that invites bitterness. Instead we should recall God's overlooking mercy toward us, in Jesus.

Third, go. If after sincere prayer and thoughtful evaluation we discern the need to reconcile, we humbly go to the person in pursuit of peace. In the case of an online offense, it's wiser to go to them in person, not online. As we go, we should be willing to shine the light of truth on both ourselves and others. This means approaching the meeting with the very real possibility that we may be wrong. It also means assuming the other party has something valuable to say.

A helpful way to start is by first praying together, asking the God of peace to bring about reconciliation. If the person refuses to pray with you, or you can't pray with her, you aren't ready for reconciliation.

Begin by sharing your own failures or sins, owning them entirely and not shifting the blame. Peace grows in the soil of meekness. Then express how you have been hurt, and listen to what the other person has to say. Remember, both of you are made in God's image and deserve respect and a listening ear. Don't interrupt. Value the person over the relationship and over being right. Give the other the benefit of the doubt. Hear him out before making a final judgment. Look to empathize and forgive, not to be right or to avoid further hurt. Instead aim to regard Christ above all things, seeking his glory, displaying his mercy, and enjoying his favor together.

It may be helpful to pray like this at the start of a meeting:

"Lord, help us to value Christ more than being right or being liked. Help us to seek your glory, to extend your mercy to one another, and to come out of this enjoying more of your favor. Amen."

It may be the case that one meeting isn't enough and that seeking peace requires more time. Remember, a peacemaker is disarming, and the ultimate goal is neither to be right nor to be liked. Instead the aim should be to cherish and reflect Christ by embracing his design for us in conflict. The peacemaker seeks the shalom of God in all situations in order for all parties to flourish. Unfortunately this approach doesn't guarantee reconciliation between people, but it does guarantee peace with God.

THE SONS OF GOD

If peaceful results are not guaranteed, why should we endure the difficult process of making peace? Because peacemakers "will be called sons of God." How is being a son of God helpful in pursuing peace? Because sons are *family*. When Yahweh rescued Israel from Egypt, he referred to his collective people as "his son" (Exodus 4:22; Hosea 11:1). Similarly, when Jesus rescues us from sin, death, and hell, he calls his people his "sons." While this may sound sexist, being called God's son is even better than gender equality. In the ancient world, it was sons, not daughters, who received the family inheritance: land, cattle, wealth, security. But now, because of faith in Jesus, all are sons. Both men and women are adopted equally into God's family to enjoy his love and receive his inheritance. As members of God's family, we are welcomed into an unmatched, inexhaustible, all-satisfying affection. This love is not based on what we have done, but on what Christ has done for us. Therefore we should extend that love to others.

As we settle into the Father's abounding love, we become less likely to demand approval from others. This frees us to enter conflict, admit wrong, and seek peace. Since the outcome of a conflict doesn't change how God feels about us or about our status in his family, his love frees us to admit our wrong and to risk rejection. We are not in fragile hands; as sons of God, we are fit with the heavenly approval necessary to seek peace with those who may disapprove of us. In the words of Peter Kreeft, "It's not that peacemaking makes you a child of God, but that being a child of God makes you a peacemaker."[13] The future reality of our sonship breaks into the present to make us peacemaking people.

A son is also an *heir*. Heir of what? The world. "For the promise to Abraham and his offspring that he would be heir of the world did not come through the law but through the righteousness of faith" (Romans 4:13). The world we will inherit is reconstituted by shalom. It's the place where the lion will lie down with the lamb, and swords will be hammered into plowshares. This new world will re-web together God, humans, and all creation in justice, fulfillment, and delight. Shalom will saturate everyone and everything.

As his sons, we will inherit the peaceful world everyone longs for. With this kind of peace in the bank, we have an endless reserve to withdraw from to make peace with others. If peace with God and a peaceful world are ours in Christ Jesus, how can we not extend peace to others?

Human beings aren't the only ones longing for this inheritance. Creation also waits eagerly, knowing that when the sons of God are revealed in their glorified, whole, sinless estate, creation too will be set free from corruption (Romans 8:19-22).

One blazing Texas summer, the earth became so dry that long, dark cracks appeared in our backyard. When we took a vacation at Lake Austin, we noticed boats marooned on the lakebed, dry docks stood on stilts, exposed. I let out a gasp. Likewise creation is gasping for healing. It longs for renewal. And it has its eye on the sons of God because it knows that when the kings and queens of creation are restored to their former glory, creation will soon follow, obtaining the freedom of the glory of the children of God. With this epic inheritance in view, it's no wonder the sons of God are peacemakers.

OVERCOMING YOUR CHAOS

- Think of a time you were tempted to participate in sinful outrage. What was the moral root behind it? Were you afraid, self-righteous, anxious?

- How can you address that sinful outrage with the hope of Christ? How can you redeem it by expressing your concern in a godlier way?

- Where have you fallen into the trap of safetyism? How has this colored the way you treat people who are different from you?

- How can you challenge the cultures of outrage and fragility by creating a culture of peace with your community?

- Do you tend to value social approval or being right more than you value a person?

- Think of a conflict that didn't end well. Apply the three circles of peacemaking to the conflict: pray, evaluate, go.

- How can you more deeply embrace your sonship in Christ?

Nine

PERSECUTION IN AN AGE OF COMFORT

"Blessed are those who are
persecuted for righteousness' sake,
for theirs is the kingdom of heaven."

MATTHEW 5:10

OVER THE PAST HUNDRED YEARS, the American workload decreased by about 50 percent.[1] During the same time, the amount of leisure time *tripled*. People used to work by day and rest by night. But in 1882 the first central power plant was opened in Lower Manhattan. By 1925, half of US homes had steady electricity. Before the distribution of electric power, people used their evenings to relax, read by candlelight, or simply turn in earlier. There was no nightlife. But with the advent of the industrial revolution and a little Red Bull, we can now play well into the night.

With expanded leisure time at our disposal, evenings have slowly become a time for entertainment rather than rest. Nightclubs, theaters, coffee shops, restaurants, and bars are now available during the old resting hours. Thanks to the innovation of streaming services, we can be entertained all night long for as little as $8.99 a month. As of 2018, Netflix alone had 118 million subscribers.

Who hasn't clicked "Next Episode" one more time, only to regret it the next day? When we sacrifice sleep for entertainment, come morning we end up hitting snooze a few more times. But late-night leisure plunders more than rest. The medium has a message. With increased entertainment comes an increased expectation of comfort: new streaming content from the comfort of our beds, people to park our cars, free refills, remote control, pizza delivery, drone package services, smart homes, and self-flushing toilets. Experiencing leisure at unprecedented levels, it's very difficult to resist the expectation of comfort and convenience.

Is it any wonder inconvenience is unwelcome? If we have to wait longer than we want for food prepared by someone else, we're easily put off. Slow Wi-Fi is unacceptable. And if Alexa doesn't get our request right the first time, we may let her have it! Speed and automation are default settings in the modern psyche. I'll admit being miffed because I had to turn the bathroom paper towel dispenser *manually* for a towel to dry my hands.

In this culture of convenience, the bar for good deeds plummets. If we allow someone to go ahead of us in line or traffic, we may feel a sudden surge of pleasure for having done a noble deed. Driving across town to deliver a homecooked meal to a sick family or new parents is downright saintly.

It is in this environment that we read, "Blessed are the persecuted." If our bar for good deeds is low, our threshold for persecution is even lower.

Ending with a chapter on persecution is fitting. We are on a razor's edge. Will we continue to compound the crisis of good in our society or instead repair the damage through humble acts of righteousness, mercy, purity, and shalom-making? To put "the good" into our crisis, we must learn how to endure persecution, grasp its challenge in an age of comfort, and live for the reward of the kingdom of heaven.

THE PERSECUTION OF COMFORT

Persecution is a "when" not an "if" for those who follow Jesus. According to Paul, "all who desire to live a godly life in Christ Jesus will be persecuted" (2 Timothy 3:12). Every generation of Christians has faced persecution. The early Christians were suspended in prominent places, soaked in oil, and torched for their faith, writhing in agony to the death. Even while living in the Holy Roman Empire, Christians faced the terror of the Barbarians. In the Middle Ages, Christians were ravaged by plagues, and during the Reformation, Protestants were persecuted by the state. Over the past two centuries, communist regimes have oppressed churches, arrested Christians, imprisoned pastors, and worse. Radical Islamic groups behead Christians in the Middle East and burn their churches in Indonesia. According to the World Christian Database, over a million Christians were martyred between 2000 and 2010.[2] What kind of persecution should we expect?

Sometimes we consider physical suffering the only true form of persecution, but when Jesus describes persecution in the Beatitudes, he includes other things: "Blessed are you when others revile you and persecute you and utter all kinds of evil against you falsely on my account. Rejoice and be glad, for your reward is great in heaven, for so they persecuted the prophets who were before you" (Matthew 5:11-12). Jesus uses three different terms to describe this persecution: revile, persecute, and speak falsely. The first, translated "revile," means to find fault as a way of shaming, to demean.[3] This form of persecution is *emotional* in nature and is intended to belittle. The second word, translated *persecute*, means to harass because of one's beliefs. It's used in the context of laying hands on a person, imprisonment, and murder (Luke 11:49; 21:12). It is *physical* in nature. The third phrase, "to speak all kinds of evil falsely," is clearly more *verbal*.

In many cases, these forms of suffering overlap, affecting mind, body, and spirit; other times they're isolated. For instance, imprisonment may be accompanied by verbal insults, while shaming may occur without a hand being laid upon us. Jesus' intention wasn't to parse out all the different types of suffering but to include a range of sufferings that constitute persecution for his sake.

While we can't rule out physical persecution in the West, we usually face a persecution that is emotional and psychological. Cultural critic and Christian apologist Ken Myers said this suffering "may be as serious for modern Christians as persecution and plagues were for the saints of earlier centuries."[4] How so? According to Myers, it is the burden of living in a consumer culture where the individual looms larger than institutions, convenience trumps self-sacrifice, and personal preference eclipses virtue. The challenge of following Jesus amid comfort is just the tip of the iceberg. Convenience has an anesthetizing effect that leaves us unaware of less-visible oppression.

When I was in college, I took a fascinating class on the anthropology of terrorism. In the class, I learned that the Japanese bombing of Pearl Harbor was planned well in advance. The Japanese waited to bomb the United States not just to catch us by surprise on an early Sunday morning without making a declaration of war, but also because the American people were *distracted*. In 1941, movies, fashion, and fast food were rapidly growing in popularity.

Despite pleas from Winston Churchill, the United States had resisted involvement in World War II. The United States and Japan had been edging toward war for decades, but our enemy struck its greatest blow when we were in the lap of luxury. Stunned by the loss of more than 2,400 lives, President Franklin D. Roosevelt quickly convened Congress and called for war. Similarly Satan has declared an attack on God's people, seeking to subvert faithfulness to Jesus through the ruse of distraction. Under his influence, we are tempted to compromise holiness for the thrills of popular culture. We would rather be served than serve.

DYING TO LIVE

A few years ago I asked my wife how I was doing serving our family. In the years leading up to that moment, my family had repeatedly asked me if we could get a dog. Each time I'd issued an emphatic "no way." For years people knew I didn't like dogs: the hair, the slobber, the constant care, the inconvenience. My dislike was so obvious that when I entered a dog owner's home, the hosts would call their dogs away from me. My wife replied to my question about my service to our family by saying, "You are great at serving our family, *as long as it's convenient.*"

That was not the reply I'd expected. I thought I would hear, "Oh, honey, you are so great at serving us. You take out the trash, discipline the kids, clean the house. You're a model of service!" So when I heard her say I serve the family as long as it's convenient, objections filled my chest. I forced out a lame excuse and said I would pray about it.

Later that week, I was reading the Gospel of John and came across Jesus saying,

> Truly, truly, I say to you, unless a grain of wheat falls into the earth and dies, it remains alone; but if it dies, it bears much fruit. Whoever loves his life loses it, and whoever hates his life in this world will keep it for eternal life. If anyone serves me, he must follow me; and where I am, there will my servant be also. (12:24-26)

Here was God's answer to my prayer: die to yourself, lose your life, serve your family. Be like Jesus. It came with a stiff warning: if you live for yourself and refuse to die, you'll end up alone in life, distant from your wife and kids, isolated in community. If the grain refuses to fall and die, it remains alone. But, if you die to self and convenience, you'll bear much fruit.

Forced to my knees in tearful repentance, I cried out for forgiveness. My unholy self came face to face with sacrificial holiness. I begged for forgiveness, not because I had to beg, but because I'd gotten a glimpse of the disparity between me and Jesus. I resolved to get a dog and began serving my family *when it was inconvenient*. I started picking up the kids when it was bad timing and fixing things around the house without being asked. Oh, and we got a dog. Did I say that already?

Without a doubt, death to self has borne fruit. My kids were filled with joy when we told them we were getting a dog. Gandalf, our poodle that looks more like a blond, shaggy labradoodle, actually likes me and I like him. He brings joy to all of us every day.

This lesson triggered many more willing sacrifices, including donating a kidney to my aunt, who was experiencing dual renal failure. When I agreed to donate a kidney, I really had no idea what I was getting into. The matching process took months, involving many trips to a transplant center in another city. During this time, medical professionals drew blood so many times I lost count. I was asked probing questions to test my psychological readiness. One question hit me like a ton of bricks, "How will you respond if the recipient's body rejects your organ?" All this sacrifice could be in vain? Then, there was the creatinine test. The test requires a twenty-four-hour urine sample in order to analyze how well your kidneys function. This means you have to pee in a bag every single time you need to go to the bathroom for a whole day and night. Oh, and the sample must be kept cool. So, I took a small orange cooler, with my urine bag in it, to work. Each time I needed to go to the restroom, I disappeared with the cooler, and then reappeared with it. Can you imagine what people were thinking? If I forgot to use the bag a single time, the whole test would have to be repeated. Guess what? I forgot, more than once.

When I woke up from the transplant surgery, I discovered the transplant was a success! But I immediately started vomiting due to an allergic reaction to the anesthesia. This was especially painful because my abdominal muscles had been sliced through to get to the kidney. I lacked the strength to get out of my own bed and go to the bathroom by myself. A catheter took care of that. Slowly I began to recover, shuffling around the nurses' station with my IV pole, as I tried to rebuild my core. I looked and felt awful. Part of my body was gone, but when it was inserted into my aunt, she gained life. Apart from the example and empowerment of Jesus—who gave way more than a kidney, and suffered the wrath of God in our place—I would never have embraced this comparatively small sacrifice.

During this season of sacrifice, I noticed my service inspired spontaneous service in other family members. Death produced life. We grew closer as a family. But the greatest fruit has been knowing Christ more. Before telling his disciples to die like a seed in the ground, Jesus said, "the hour has come for the Son of Man to be glorified" (John 12:23, speaking of his death). The hour of his death was the hour of his glory. Now *that* is countercultural. The cross comes before the crown, the way up is down, no servant is greater than his master.

Every day we imbibe a message that says just the opposite, "Indulge for glory." Jesus says, "Die and you will truly live," and he backs it up with his very own life. What God requires, he provides. We can die to ourselves because Jesus died first. And his death didn't end in death—nor will ours. Resurrection glory awaits those who take up their cross and follow Jesus. The fruit of new creation is promised to all who follow him. Glimpsing this vision of Christ, I have been freed to confess my love of convenience, to enjoy forgiveness, and to serve, even when it's inconvenient. I am still learning.

INVISIBLE PERSECUTION

Another difficulty in following Jesus in a culture of comfort is the fear of missing out. Instead of sacrifice or willing persecution, we often plunge ourselves into serial consumer experiences. If we aren't up on the box-office hits, we may feel out of step in small talk. If a new restaurant pops up, and we haven't visited it within the first three months, we may feel on the out with all the cool kids. There's also a pull to stay up with the latest fashion, craft coffee, beer, and Apple products. (Sorry, Android users.) We swim in incessant appeals to consume, not only for satisfaction but also for social approval. If we fail to stay up with consumer culture, we might just be left behind—or at least lose some clout. Pumped full of the latest and greatest, or pining for more, we blend in with those around us. There's no visible reason to persecute comfortable Christians. Their lifestyle poses no threat. Their beliefs are indiscernibly different from everyone else's.

Under the anesthesia of consumer culture, secularism takes its cut.[5] The facts are in. The number of people who no longer identify with a religion has tripled in the United States over the past fifteen years. Thirty-seven percent of religious nones say their reason for leaving religion is "unbelief in God." Sixty percent say it's because they "question a lot of religious teachings."[6] Disassociated with some of its rich, gospel-centered heritage, "evangelical" has been reduced to a right-wing, sometimes racist, political voting bloc. Is it any wonder the nones question a lot of religious teaching? Instead of suffering for righteousness' sake, some Christians are persecuted for unrighteousness' sake.

When attending his son's funeral, Vice President Joe Biden was greeted by a "Christian" group holding signs that read, "Thank God for dead soldiers. God hates Fag enablers." These so-called Christians chose not to "weep with those who weep" (Romans 12:15), but to exploit Biden's mourning with their hatred. In turn, a bystander threw hot coffee on the group.

Make no mistake, those picketers weren't being persecuted for righteousness' sake but for unrighteousness' sake. Jesus doesn't throw blanket blessings on Christians irrespective of their behavior. He doesn't condone self-righteous culture-war crusaders, racist white supremacy groups, or smug holier-than-thou folks. Jesus promised blessing for humble, righteous allegiance to him: "Blessed are you when others revile you and persecute you and utter all kinds of evil against you falsely on my account" (Matthew 5:11). Persecution on his account is suffering that stems from humble allegiance to Jesus and his teachings.

The self-centered values of consumer culture have made it difficult to follow Jesus in the twenty-first-century West. But is this comparable to the burnings of the saints? Myers says it may actually be harder, since "enemies that come loudly and visibly are usually much easier to fight than those that are undetectable."[7]

Physical persecution is a clear summons to faith, but invisible persecution is a subtle and slow subversion of faith.

Is it any wonder that the center of global Christianity has shifted from the West to the South and the East? Comfort elicits a love of convenience; convenience lowers the bar of sacrifice; and indulgent Christians lack the faith and character required to follow Jesus. In fact, we're tempted to downplay or hide our faith in Jesus, adoring the approval of peers more than we enjoy the love of God.

Invisible persecution in a secular age reveals true and false faith. Some fritter away their days immersed in distraction, without anything to show King Jesus when he returns. They will suffer loss, having all of their works consumed by fire, though narrowly being saved (1 Corinthians 3:15). Others won't make it through the fire of judgment at all, since they've settled for the comforts of the world while parading a hollow, politicized faith and a costless discipleship. But Jesus promised blessing to those who possess humble allegiance to him.

HUMBLE ALLEGIANCE

What does humble allegiance to Jesus and his teachings look like in an age of comfort? It looks like Jesus. Those who are persecuted for Christ's sake resemble Christ. It isn't enough to take Christ's name. Near the end of his sermon, Jesus said something absolutely penetrating: "Not everyone who says to me, 'Lord, Lord,' will enter the kingdom of heaven" (Matthew 7:21). It isn't enough to *believe* Jesus is Lord, although that is a radical and true claim in its own right. For the Jews, confessing Jesus as Lord meant believing that Jesus shares in Yahweh's full deity and power. This was a radical step. Making this claim in the Roman Empire meant going even further, challenging Caesar's claim to lordship. Bold and true, belief in Jesus was dangerous for Jews, Greeks, and Romans.

Today insisting on exclusive allegiance to Jesus as the one true God and Savior of humanity is also radical. It's a declaration of war against the cult of expressive individualism. It's unpopular to denounce the self, but it isn't enough to confess Jesus as Lord. His lordship must be visible. It isn't enough to have great theology about Jesus and claim him as your king. It isn't enough to say he is *the* God and there is no other. Rather our allegiance to him must be evident in our character and action. We must care for the poor, practice righteousness, seek purity, and make peace with others. The Beatitudes of Jesus must define us.

Alternatively, it isn't enough to look like Jesus, for he says, "On that day many will say to me, 'Lord, Lord, did we not prophesy in your name, and cast out demons in your name, and do many mighty works in your name?' And then will I declare to them, 'I never knew you; depart from me, you workers of lawlessness'" (Matthew 7:22-23). It isn't enough to resemble Christ in preaching, teaching, and small-group discussions. It isn't adequate to be a spiritual warrior who fasts, prays, and exorcises. Nor is it satisfactory to do mighty works of justice and mercy, such as working for racial justice, gender equality, and rights for the unborn. We must be poor *in spirit*, cling to the righteousness *of Christ*, cultivate purity *of heart*, rest in the mercy *of God*, and bank on the shalom *of the cross*. The Jesus of the Beatitudes must define us.

Jesus is after humble allegiance to *himself*. This doesn't mean merely including Jesus in our bio or on our bumper, though those are fine. It doesn't even mean that we love Jesus, although that is necessary. It means *banking our reputation on the fact that Jesus loves us*. It's risking the approval of others by telling them the truth of the gospel, while resting in the approval of God's love for us in Christ. Our allegiance to Jesus is in response to his unqualified commitment to us. We stand not on a shred of *our* theology or *our* good works, but on the life, death, resurrection, and return of Jesus *for us*.

When we take this in, it should make us humble. We're profoundly known and loved *by* God. This should also make us loving, patient, and kind toward others, even those who are radically different. But to those who cling to a name—"Lord, Lord"—or declare their good works, Jesus said, "I never knew you."

Let that sink in. Jesus must *know* us. He must be able to see the family resemblance: *his* righteousness, *his* mercy, *his* peace, as we extend it all to others. In short, we are called to be a foretaste of the kingdom of heaven.

THE KINGDOM OF HEAVEN

What will motivate us to embrace sacrifice in a culture of comfort? What will keep us from abandoning Jesus and his teachings when friends misunderstand or desert us? We need a source of greater comfort and joy. We need the kingdom of heaven.

The kingdom of true comfort. Although the kingdom of heaven is a Spirit-filled learning community, it is much more. It is a kingdom of true comfort. Heaven is a place where *every* tear is wiped away by the hand of God (Revelation 21:4; 7:17).

This doesn't mean that Jesus will be there for every tear with Kleenex, but that he will remove the need for them entirely! He will dispense with the agent of evil by tossing him into a lake of fire where he "will be tormented day and night forever and ever" (Revelation 20:10). The threat of sorrow is removed *permanently*.

This is also why Revelation describes the kingdom as a place where "the sea was no more" (21:1). In the ancient world, the sea was a place of unpredictable, life-threatening chaos. The sailors who transported Jonah feared for their lives in the storm, and the disciples of Jesus were fraught with fear in the squall that whipped up on the Sea of Galilee. But in the kingdom of heaven, the Lord of the seas banishes all storms. His reign breaks in on earth too, for "he awoke and rebuked the wind and said to the sea, 'Peace! Be still!' And the wind ceased, and there was a great calm" (Mark 4:39). The Greek word for "be still" means to muzzle. The Lord Jesus muzzles what terrifies us. Everything that produces pain and sorrow is on a leash. He restrains and permits suffering to drive us to true comfort.

Prior to the squall, the shuddering disciples didn't know Jesus as the Prince of Peace. They knew him as a great teacher, an exorcist, and a close friend. They even knew the secrets of the kingdom of God, explained by Jesus himself. But they lacked an existential knowledge of Jesus as Lord of the seas, the Prince of Peace and Mighty God. Only by weathering the storm could they learn the inestimable value of their sleeping passenger. They conclude, "Who then is this, that even the wind and the sea obey him?" (Mark 4:41). The disciples discovered a comfort greater than their fears by going *through the storm* with Jesus.

Jesus wants to reveal more of his immensity and grandeur to us in our sufferings, knowing it will furnish us with inexplicable comfort and joy. Jesus blesses those who mourn with a comfort so deep and so true it eclipses our sorrow. He gives us more than "meaning"; he gives us *himself*—the eternal, portable, faithful companionship of God. Nothing but the kingdom of heaven can offer that.

The kingdom of joy. The kingdom of heaven also offers us a joy that outstrips what friends and comforts can offer us. Jesus put joy and heaven together in this Beatitude when he said, "Rejoice and be glad, for your reward is great in heaven" (Matthew 5:12). What is this reward that makes joy leap from heaven to earth? It's so immense, so rich and full, so multi-dimensional in its glory and immeasurable in its felicity, I can't adequately describe it. In fact, commentators Albright and Mann note, "the reward is so far beyond anything which men could possibly attain by their own goodness that the very word *reward* has something of an irony about it."[8] For this reason, let's allow a few images from the book of Revelation to help us grasp the joy of heaven.

THE REWARDS OF REVELATION

The tree of life. In his letters to the seven churches, Jesus promised reward to those who "conquer" or overcome perse-cution in faithfulness to him. To the church in Ephesus, he promised the right to eat from "the tree of life, which is in the paradise of God" (Revelation 2:7). This reward symbolizes the joy not just of eternal life but also of never-ending life in a renewed creation. As Frankenstein's immortal monster attested, it would be an eternal misery to live forever in the world as it is: "My life, as it passed thus, was indeed hateful to me, and it was during sleep alone that I could taste joy. O blessed sleep! often, when most miserable, I sank to repose, and my dreams lulled me even to rapture."[9]

Joy is but a dream when trapped in a hideous, carnal life. But the tree promises a life in the paradise of God, the world remade in resplendent beauty, goodness, and justice, where no unclean thing or person will enter. The new creation is a cosmos fit for the eternal King, and our reward is to *belong* there forever. Our eternal life will not be merely quantitative (a life that never ends) but also qualitative (a life suffused with joy because of eternal citizenship in the kingdom of Christ). These images promise never-ending, never-fading life in God's new creation.

A *white stone* and *hidden manna.* To the church in Pergamum, Jesus promised "hidden manna" and a "white stone" with a new name written on it (Revelation 2:17). The manna is likely an allusion to our place at the table of feasting at the marriage supper of the Lamb. This heavenly food is an image of *unhindered fellowship with Jesus.* We won't sheepishly drag ourselves to the table; we'll take our place confidently next to the Lord Christ, brimming with joy, because we have a new name only he knows.

Not only has he called us by name, but he has renamed us to fit his call. We belong at the table and have a white rock to prove it. A black stone indicated guilt, but a white stone was associated with acquittal. We can savor every bite in the presence of the King because we have been acquitted of every wrong. Guilt and shame have no place at his table—only endless joy. These images promise unhindered, shameless fellow-ship with Jesus.

Sitting on the throne. And to the one who overcomes lukewarm faith, the church at Ephesus, Jesus promised the right to—get this—"sit with me on my throne, as I also conquered and sat down with my Father on his throne" (Revelation 3:21). The first time I read this verse, my shoulders slumped and my head dropped, as my forehead plowed into my Bible. Sit with Jesus on his throne? The King of kings and the Lord of lords? Surely this is a typo?!

It is not. To sit on Christ's throne is not to subvert his reign or to take his place but to step into the *rightful inheritance* of God's new creation. In the words of Paul, we become coheirs with Christ (Romans 8:17). We so deserve to be in the new creation that we can sit on its regent's throne. God the Father will not chase us away from the seat, as if we were pesky children who don't belong. Rather we will sit *with* Christ on *his* throne. Make no mistake, it is *his* throne, and we are sitting in his lap. So picture yourself in his magnificent lap, settled into his affectionate embrace, looking out over the gleaming, renewed cosmos that is the kingdom of heaven, and think to yourself, *This is mine.* This image promises belonging and rightful inheritance in the paradise of God.

All of this can be yours: the tree of life, the hidden manna, the white stone, a place on the throne in the paradise of God, a never-ending life in a renewed creation, unhindered fellowship with Jesus, and a rightful inheritance of the paradise of God. We need only to persevere in faith.

But what if I stumble? Don't worry, the King was pinned to the tree of death to give us new life.

What if I demand meat instead of manna? Fret not, for Christ is the bread of life. Bite down on his sacrificial sustenance.

What if I cast disrepute on his name? Repent and run back to the one who gives you a new name.

Endurance in persecution is not a call to overnight perfection but to humble, persevering allegiance to Jesus over a lifetime. Oh joy of joys to be found in Christ, redefined by his name, his perseverance, and his triumph! Oh, death, where is your sting?

This felicitous future is promised to those who put their faith in the Lord of the Beatitudes, not in the Beatitudes themselves. It's a future that breaks into the present. For we eat at his table *now*, enjoy his fellowship, bear his name, and serve in his kingdom. Surely this is an indescribable comfort and a joy: a celestial kingdom placed in our chests, waiting to burst forth in acts of mercy, mourning, purity, righteousness, and shalom.

May this goodness be increasingly visible as we labor to put Christ on display in a world in crisis, for a bright, new world is coming, a future as bright as the promises of God.[10]

OVERCOMING YOUR CHAOS

- ◆ How has convenience and comfort lowered your bar for persecution? Think of specific ways you are lured by comfort at the expense of service.
- ◆ Read John 12:24-26. In what ways might Christ be calling you to die and bear much fruit? Make this a matter of prayer and reflection.

- How can you embrace sacrifice for the fame of Jesus? For the good of your community or church?
- Which of these images of the kingdom of heaven (the tree of life, the hidden manna, the white stone, a place on the throne) is most appealing to you? Why? How can you take that image with you to motivate sacrifice and service?
- How does Jesus help us endure persecution?

EPILOGUE

OUTSPOKEN ATHEIST RICHARD DAWKINS was right. The Sermon on the Mount was way ahead of its time—but not merely because of its ethical superiority. The Beatitudes radiate with wisdom and beauty because they come from outside time—from the future, so to speak—where God dwells. God unfurls his moral excellence in these stunning statements of blessing. Each one presents the possibility of a world rid of moral chaos. The Beatitudes are a vision of the kingdom of heaven breaking into earth, populated with the meek and the just, the pure and the true.

This is also more than a divine vision; it's the Father's pledge, backed by the blood of his Son, secured by his own Spirit. God is making heavenly men and women, not merely through moral conformity to himself but through mystical union with Christ. The Beatitudes are invitations to walk closely with our Savior on pathways into his manifold perfections. They begin with poverty and end in reward.

The way into the mystical, inebriating love of Christ is not through moral perfection but humble reflection. It is by acknowledging our need, not announcing our plenty, that we gain access to the Son. Isaiah said it well: "But to this one I will look,

To him who is humble and contrite of spirit, and who trembles at My word" (Isaiah 66:2 NASB). Will you tremble at Christ's holy character inscribed in these sayings? Will you reach out, not ultimately for virtue but for help? Then salvation will come and righteousness with it. Christ will answer our cry, every time. His face does not cease to shine nor his mercies tarnish. They are new every morning.

Each Beatitude inspires and challenges us at once; together they beckon us to a future garden where loving will be like walking and righteousness falls like rain. Until then, we must see our sin and evil through the eyes of our suffering Savior, where the comfort of heaven overlaps the sufferings of earth. Take heart, and keep your eyes on Christ. Dig in, and walk in his ways. Endure, for reward is coming. See Christ with the eyes of faith, and his glory will become visible to those around you. Droplets of his beauty will roll off us, causing goodness to spring up around us.

When we do this together, we nourish the world with Jesus' coherent and fruitful moral vision. When we're absorbed with Christ, the Spirit puts the future on display, in advance, and people get a glimpse of the kingdom of heaven.

ACKNOWLEDGMENTS

MY SINCEREST THANKS TO MY EDITORS, Cindy Bunch and Ethan McCarthy, who gave helpful feedback and shared encouraging notes along the way. I'm also grateful to my brother, Luke Dodson, who believed in this book from the beginning and refined my thinking through our engaging conversations at Caffe Medici. Special thanks to my wife, Robie, and my kids, Owen, Ellie, and Rosamund, who supported me in this project and patiently love me through the ups and downs of life. You guys are awesome! Finally, Jesus, thank you for coming to earth not only to teach us the sparkling wisdom of the Beatitudes but also to live them flawlessly on our behalf.

NOTES

CHAPTER 1: FLOURISHING
IN AN AGE OF CRISIS

[1]Amy is a pseudonym.

[2]If you have had an abortion and suffer from the guilt and shame that often follows, or if you want to understand how to help someone who has struggled with these complex thoughts and painful emotions, I recommend you read the account of a woman who had two abortions and how she dealt with them, Christine Hoover, "In Her Shoes: One Woman's Testimony is about Abortion and God's Grace" *JBC* 29, no. 2 (2015): 36–44. The article can be accessed here: www.ccef.org/shop/product/shoes-one-womans-testimony -abortion-gods-grace.

[3]Looking back on my sin and its consequences is humbling. I have sought and felt God's forgiveness for my sin. I have contemplated that fork-in-the road decision many times. Although I would have made a different decision had I known then what I know now, I have come to trust in the wise providence of God over these actions, "The lot is cast into the lap, but every decision is from the LORD" (Prov 16:33). While we are responsible for our moral actions, as we will see in this book, God is simultaneously sovereign over them, guiding them into a complex, inscrutable story of redemption and grace. I am responsible; he is sovereign. I have sinned; he has forgiven me. I am a mess; he is nuts about me in Jesus. This is my hope, and it is yours too.

[4]Aristotle, *Politics*, 1253a, 35.

[5]Some of the passages I have cited convey the notion of judgment by using the word *krisis* (in the Septuagint, the Greek translation of the Old Testament), such as Judges 4:4-5. Others convey judgment through the imagery of the tree and actions surrounding it.

[6]Reinhart Koselleck and Michaela W. Richter, "Crisis," *Journal of the History of Ideas* 67, no. 2 (April 2006): 357-400, www.jstor.org/stable/30141882.

[7]Koselleck and Richter, 399.

[8]Daniel Patrick Moynihan, "An American Original," *Vanity Fair*, November 2010, www.vanityfair.com/news/2010/11/moynihan-letters-201011.

[9]Dallas Willard, *The Disappearance of Moral Knowledge* (New York: Routledge, 2018), 6. Willard identified six contributing factors to the sudden change in the zeitgeist: (1) discrediting of religion as a source of knowledge, (2) disappearance of human self, (3) cultural variations in morality, (4) moral standards seen as power plays, (5) morality seen as harmful, (6) resentment of knowledge.

[10]When I was young, my British grandparents lived in Brighton, England. I remember getting this candy from them, but I borrow the third illustration from N. T. Wright, *After You Believe: Why Christian Character Matters* (New York: HarperCollins, 2010), 27.

[11]Paul Farhi, "'Today' show host Matt Lauer fired after claims of 'inappropriate sexual behavior,'" *Washington Post*, November 29, 2017, www.washingtonpost .com/lifestyle/style/today-show-host-matt-lauer-fired-after-claims-of -inappropriate-sexual-behavior/2017/11/29/ee85bf42-d4fd-11e7-b62d -d9345ced896d_story.html.

[12]Joshua Hawley, "Are American Evangelicals Stingy?," *Christianity Today*, January 31, 2011, www.christianitytoday.com/ct/2011/february/areevan gelicalsstingy.html.

[13]Joshua Pease, "The sin of silence: The epidemic of denial about sexual abuse in the evangelical church," *The Washington Post*, May 31, 2018, www .washingtonpost.com/news/posteverything/wp/2018/05/31/feature/the -epidemic-of-denial-about-sexual-abuse-in-the-evangelical-church/?utm _term=.947d144f0ab5.

[14]Richard Dawkins, *The God Delusion* (New York: Houghton-Mifflin, 2006), 250.

[15]This quote is often attributed to Pelikan; however, the closest quote I can find to it refers to the Sermon on the Mount as "the greatest of all sermons," Jaroslav Pelikan, *Divine Rhetoric: The Sermon on the Mount As Message and As Model in Augustine, Chrysostom, and Luther* (Crestwood, NY: St Vladimir's Seminary Press, 2000), 102.

[16]Jonathan T. Pennington, *The Sermon on the Mount and Human Flourishing* (Grand Rapids: Baker, 2017), 35.

[17]For an excellent treatment of the future logic of the New Testament see Richard Hays, *The Moral Vision of the New Testament* (New York: Harper Collins, 1996).

[18]Pennington, *The Sermon*, 40; Scot McKnight, *Sermon on the Mount* (Grand Rapids: Zondervan, 2013), 8-14.

[19]Kendrick Lamar and U2, "American Soul," *Songs of Experience* CD, December 2017.

[20]In the categories of Charles Taylor, I am leaning on the "sense 3" meaning of secularity, in which belief in God becomes increasingly difficult and contested. Taylor writes, "The shift to secularity in this sense consists, among other things, of a move from a society where belief in God is unchallenged and indeed, unproblematic, to one in which it is understood to be one option among others, and frequently not the easiest to embrace." Taylor, *A Secular Age* (Cambridge, MA: Belknap Press, 2007), 3.

[21]I have borrowed the term "the Big Me" from the insightful and inspiring book by David Brooks, *The Road to Character* (New York: Random House, 2015), 240-70.

CHAPTER 2: POOR IN SPIRIT
IN AN AGE OF THE BIG ME

[1]See Alfred T. Hennelly, *Liberation Theology: A Documentary History* (Maryknoll, NY: Orbis, 1990), chaps. 10, 12.

[2]Tom Wolfe, "The 'Me' Decade and the Third Great Awakening," *New York Magazine*, August 23, 1976, 13.

[3]Wolfe, "The 'Me' Decade," 13.

[4]Dallas Willard, *The Divine Conspiracy: Rediscovering Our Hidden Life in God* (San Francisco: HarperCollins, 1998), 102. While our experience of this shift in moral reasoning may seem sudden, ethicists have traced the history of emotivism, the belief that all judgments and morals are simply expressions of feeling or preference. For a helpful discussion, see Alasdair MacIntyre, *After Virtue: A Study in Moral Theory* (Notre Dame: University of Notre Dame Press, 1994), 6-35.

[5]Scot McKnight, *Sermon on the Mount* (Grand Rapids: Zondervan, 2013), 39.

[6]McKnight, *Sermon*, 40.

[7]Martyn Lloyd-Jones, *Studies in the Sermon on the Mount* (Grand Rapids: Eerdmans, 1960), 33, 40.

[8]Brooks describes a person of character this way: "They radiate a sort of moral joy. . . . They answer softly when challenged harshly. They are silent when unfairly abused. . . . But they get things done. . . . They are not thinking about what impressive work they are doing. They are not thinking about themselves at all. . . . They are the people who have built strong inner character." David Brooks, *The Road to Character* (New York: Random House, 2015), xvi-xvii.

[9]Christopher Lasch discusses Rubin in his *The Culture of Narcissism* (New York: Norton, 1979), 14-15.

[10]Cited in Lasch, *The Culture of Narcissism*, 14.

[11]Lasch, *The Culture of Narcissism*, 17.

[12]Lasch, *The Culture of Narcissism*, 6.

[13]Some of these insights on the divided self and the mask imagery come from J. Richard Middleton and Brian J. Walsh, *The Truth Is Stranger Than It Used to Be* (Downers Grove, IL: InterVarsity Press, 1995), 154.

[14]Broken Bells, "Perfect World," *After the Disco*, Columbia Records, 2014.

[15]"Cigna's U.S. Loneliness Index," Cigna, May 1, 2018, www.multivu.com /players/English/8294451-cigna-us-loneliness-survey.

[16]Sabrina Tavernise, "U.S. Suicide Rate Surges to a 30-Year High," *New York Times*, www.nytimes.com/2016/04/22/health/us-suicide-rate-surges-to-a-30 -year-high.html.

[17]"Suicide rates rising across the U.S.," Centers for Disease Control and Prevention, June 7, 2018, www.cdc.gov/media/releases/2018/p0607 -suicide-prevention.html.

[18]Lloyd-Jones, *Sermon on the Mount*, 40.

[19]Shakespeare, Hamlet, act 3, scene 4, "The Queen's Closet," Open Source Shakespeare, www.opensourceshakespeare.org/views/plays/play_view.php ?WorkID=hamlet&Act=3&Scene=4&Scope=scene.

CHAPTER 3: MOURNING
IN AN AGE OF DISTRACTION

[1]Jeffrey Gottfried and Michael Barthel, "Almost seven-in-ten Americans have news fatigue, more among Republicans," Pew Research Center, June 5, 2018, www.pewresearch.org/fact-tank/2018/06/05/almost-seven -in-ten-americans-have-news-fatigue-more-among-republicans/.

[2]Cited in Peter Kreeft, *Back to Virtue* (Nashville: Thomas Nelson, 1996), 125.

[3]Victor Frankl, *Man's Search for Meaning* (Boston: Beacon Press, 2006).

[4]Frankl, *Man's Search*, 113.

[5]Cited in Carl Honoré, *In Praise of Slowness* (New York: HarperCollins, 2004), 4.

[6]Claudia Wallis, "The Multitasking Generation," *Time*, March 27, 2006, 53.

[7]Nicholas Carr, *The Shallows* (New York: Norton, 2010), 116.

[8]Marshall McLuhan, *Understanding Media: The Extensions of Man* (New York: Mentor Books, 1964), 23-35.

[9]Cited in David Brooks, *The Road to Character* (New York: Random House, 2015), 94.

[10]*Paraklētos* occurs only five times in the New Testament, all in Johannine literature. Four times it refers to the Holy Spirit and once to Jesus Christ. It has been difficult for scholars to come to a solid consensus in translating the word. Translations range from *advocate* to *comforter*. Discerning a latent trinitarian theology in John's use of the word, Edward Klink concluded, "Jesus and now the Spirit witness to God, speak on behalf of God, console, guide, and teach in the way of God, and help in the work of God." See the discussion in Edward W. Klink, *John: An Exegetical Commentary* (Grand Rapids: Zondervan, 2016), 631-35.

[11]C. S. Lewis, *The Great Divorce* (New York: Macmillan, 1946), 67.

[12]C. S. Lewis, *The Great Divorce*, 27.

CHAPTER 4: MEEKNESS
IN AN AGE OF HUBRIS

[1]"A Portrait of 'Generation Next,'" Pew Research Center, January 9, 2007, www.people-press.org/2007/01/09/a-portrait-of-generation-next.

[2]In their culturally prescient album *Delusions of Grand Fur*, Rogue Wave sings over and over, "Look at me / Look at me / Look at me."

[3]C. S. Lewis, *Mere Christianity* (New York: HarperCollins, 2009), 122.

[4]Ernest Hemingway, "In Another Country," in *Men Without Women* (New York: Scribner, 1997), 46.

[5]G. K. Chesterton, *Orthodoxy* (New York: Garden City, 1959), 31-32.

[6]Masha Gessen, "The Putin Paradigm," NYR Daily, December 13, 1996. Cited in Michiko Kakutani, *The Death of Truth: Notes on Falsehood in the Age of Trump* (New York: Tim Duggan Books, 2018), 96.

[7]Martyn Lloyd-Jones, *Studies in the Sermon on the Mount* (Grand Rapids: Eerdmans, 1959–60), 57.

[8]David Dark, "The Context of Love Is the World: Liturgies of Incarceration," *Comment* 34, no. 1 (March 3, 2016): 12-17.

[9]Dark, "The Context of Love."

CHAPTER 5: RIGHTEOUSNESS IN AN AGE OF VALUES

[1]C. S. Lewis, *The Abolition of Man* (New York: HarperCollins, 2006).

[2]David Brooks, *The Road to Character* (New York: Random House, 2015), 31.

[3]Mark Bauerlein, "A Crisis of Credibility," *First Things*, August, 8, 2018, www.firstthings.com/blogs/firstthoughts/2018/08/a-crisis-of-credibility.

[4]Glenn Kessler and Meg Kelly, "President Trump Made 2,140 False or Misleading Claims in His First Year," *Washington Post*, January 10, 2018.

[5]Dallas Willard, *The Disappearance of Moral Knowledge* (New York: Routledge, 2018), 44.

[6]Phil Zuckerman, *Living the Secular Life* (New York: Penguin, 2014), 13.

[7]Zuckerman, *Living the Secular Life*, 13.

[8]See Timothy Keller's helpful chapter, "Why Can't I Be Free to Life as I See Fit, as Long as I Don't Harm Anyone," in *Making Sense of God* (New York: Viking Press, 2016), 97-117.

[9]Contributing author Nancy deClaisse-Walford comments in Nancy deClaisse-Walford, R. A. Jacobson, and B. Tanner, *Book One of the Psalter: Psalms 1–41*, 2014, in E. J. Young, R. K. Harrison, and R. L. Hubbard Jr., eds., *The Book of Psalms* (Grand Rapids: Eerdmans, 2014), 189.

[10]Andrew Sullivan, "Andrew Sullivan: Christianity in Crisis," *Newsweek*, April 4, 2012, https://www.newsweek.com/andrew-sullivan-christianity-crisis-64025.

[11]This is not to say, however, that same-sex attraction or medically necessary abortions are sinful. We must distinguish the effects of the fall from willful, fallen actions. Certainly, both issues of homosexuality and abortion require nuanced ethical reasoning and sensitive pastoral care. Unfortunately, some churches take rigid stances, to the right and to the left, without careful examination of Scripture and thoughtful care for others. For thoughtful examples on these topics see, Rosaria Butterfield, *Openness Unhindered: Further Thoughts of an Unlikely Convert on Sexual Identity and Union with Christ* (Pittsburgh: Crown & Covenant, 2015); Scott Klusendorf, *The Case*

for Life (Wheaton, IL: Crossway, 2009); Christopher Kaczor, *The Ethics of Abortion* (New York: Routledge, 2014).

[12]Gary Gutting, "Returning to the Sermon on the Mount," *New York Times*, April 19, 2012, https://opinionator.blogs.nytimes.com/2012/04/19/returning -to-the-sermon-on-the-mount/.

[13]Michael Warren Davis, "Andy Warhol's devotion was almost surreal," *Catholic Herald*, February 8, 2018, catholicherald.co.uk/issues/february-9th -2018/andy-warhols-devotion-was-almost-surreal.

CHAPTER 6: MERCY IN AN AGE OF TOLERANCE

[1]This is a description of the new tolerance, which sees all views as equally valid. However, classical tolerance sees all views not as equally valid but as all having the right to exist. Classical tolerance grants dignity to other views without making the illogical assumption that they are true. It respects the individual without disrespecting the search for what is true. I am critiquing the new tolerance. This way of categorizing tolerance comes from D. A. Carson, *The Intolerance of Tolerance* (Grand Rapids: Eerdmans, 2012), 3. For further discussion, see Jonathan Dodson, *The Unbelievable Gospel: Say Something Worth Believing* (Grand Rapids: Zondervan, 2014), 67-72.

[2]"Haverhill man arrested after allegedly working out nude at Plaistow gym," Boston 25 News, July 23, 2018, www.boston25news.com/news/haverhill -man-arrested-after-allegedly-working-out-nude-at-plaistow-gym/796567618.

[3]Chris Wright, "Plato's Just State," *Philosophy Now*, 2012, philosophynow. org/issues/90/Platos_Just_State.

[4]Karen Swallow Prior, *On Reading Well: Finding the Good Life through Great Books* (Grand Rapids: Brazos, 2018), 85.

[5]Often we speak of God's love as unconditional, as though there are no conditions upon his love. However, David Powlison makes the point that God is more profound—that it is against or "contra" the conditions of our rebellious indifference. See Powlison, *God's Love: Better Than Unconditional* (Philipsburg, New Jersey: P&R, 2001).

CHAPTER 7: PURITY IN AN AGE OF SELF-EXPRESSION

[1]See You Be You's website: www.youbeyou.co.uk/projects.

[2]Robert N. Bellah, *Habits of the Heart: Individualism and Commitment in American Life* (Los Angeles: University of California Press, 1996), 333-34.

[3]Cited in David Wells, *The Courage to Be Protestant: Reformation Faith in Today's World*, 2nd ed. (Grand Rapids: Eerdmans, 2016), 129.

[4]Kim Severson, "For Larger Customers, Eating Out is Still a Daunting Experience," *New York Times*, March 12, 2019, www.nytimes.com/2019/03/12/dining/larger-customers-restaurants.html.

[5]Benjamin Weiser, "Ross Ulbricht, Creator of Silk Road Website, Is Sentenced to Life in Prison," *New York Times*, May 29, 2015, www.nytimes.com/2015/05/30/nyregion/ross-ulbricht-creator-of-silk-road-website-is-sentenced-to-life-in-prison.html.

[6]Weiser, "Ross Ulbricht."

[7]Dietrich Bonhoeffer, *The Cost of Discipleship* (London: SCM Press, 1959), 79.

[8]George Hawley, "What Americans Think About Open Marriages," *The American Conservative*, May 16, 2017, www.theamericanconservative.com/articles/what-americans-think-about-open-marriages.

[9]Alexandr Solzhenitsyn, *The Gulag Archipelago Abridged* (New York: Harper, 2007), 75.

[10]Martyn Lloyd-Jones, *Studies in the Sermon on the Mount* (Grand Rapids: Eerdmans, 1960), 92.

[11]Louis Berkof, *Systematic Theology* (Grand Rapids: Banner of Truth, 1996), 65.

CHAPTER 8: PEACEMAKING
IN AN AGE OF OUTRAGE

[1]Teddy Wayne, "Clicking Their Way to Outrage," *New York Times*, July 3, 2014, www.nytimes.com/2014/07/06/fashion/social-media-some-susceptible-to-internet-outrage.html.

[2]Wayne, "Clicking Their Way."

[3]Sarah Mervosh and Emily S. Rueb, "Fuller Picture Emerges of Viral Video of Native American Man and Catholic Students," *New York Times*, January 20, 2019, www.nytimes.com/2019/01/20/us/nathan-phillips-covington.html. In exemplary fashion, Sandmann went on to say, "I am a faithful Christian and practicing Catholic, and I always try to live up to the ideals my faith teaches me—to remain respectful of others, and to take no action that would lead to conflict or violence. . . . I harbor no ill will for this person. . . . I respect this person's right to protest and engage in free speech activities, and I support his chanting on the steps of the Lincoln

Memorial any day of the week. I believe he should re-think his tactics of invading the personal space of others, but that is his choice to make."

[4]Nelson Mandela, *In His Own Words* (New York: Little, Brown, 2003), 545.

[5]Greg Lukianoff and Jonathan Haidt, *The Coddling of the American Mind* (New York: Penguin, 2018), 30.

[6]Lukianoff and Haidt, *The Coddling*, 54.

[7]Lukianoff and Haidt, *The Coddling*, 54.

[8]I put *victim* and *oppressor* in quotes, not to suggest that there are never any true victims or oppressors—indeed there are—but to draw attention to this reductionist, uncharitable categorization of people.

[9]Cited in Lukianoff and Haidt, *The Coddling*, 50.

[10]Chris McGreal, "Rwanda Genocide 20 Years On," *The Guardian*, May 12, 2013, www.theguardian.com/world/2013/may/12/rwanda-genocide-20 -years-on.

[11]Cornelius Plantinga, *Not the Way It's Supposed to Be: A Breviary of Sin* (Grand Rapids: Eerdmans, 1996), 10.

[12]McGreal, "Rwanda Genocide 20 Years On."

[13]Peter Kreeft, *Back to Virtue* (Nashville: Thomas Nelson, 1996), 147.

CHAPTER 9: PERSECUTION
IN AN AGE OF COMFORT

[1]Paul Heintzman, *Leisure and Spirituality: Biblical, Historical, and Contemporary Perspectives* (Grand Rapids: Baker Academic, 2015), xvi.

[2]Todd M. Johnson and Gina A. Zurlo, eds. *World Christian Database* (Leiden/ Boston: Brill, 2018). https://worldchristiandatabase.org/updates.

[3]I have summarized these definitions from Walter Bauer, et al., *A Greek-English Lexicon of the New Testament and Other Early Christian Literature*, 3rd ed. (Chicago: University of Chicago Press, 2000).

[4]Ken Myers, *All God's Children and Blue Suede Shoes: Christians and Popular Culture* (Wheaton, IL: Crossway, 1989), v.

[5]"America's Changing Religious Landscape," *Pew Research Center*, May 12, 2015, www.pewforum.org/2015/05/12/americas-changing-religious-landscape/.

[6]Becka Alper, "Why America's 'nones' don't identify with a religion," *Pew Research Center*, August 8, 2018, www.pewresearch.org/fact-tank/2018/08/08 /why-americas-nones-dont-identify-with-a-religion/.

[7]Ken Myers, *All God's Children and Blue Suede Shoes*, xiii.

[8]W. F. Albright and C. S. Mann, *Matthew*, The Anchor Bible (New York: Yale, 1971) cited in Leon Morris, *The Gospel of Matthew* (Grand Rapids: Eerdmans, 1992), 103.

[9]Mary Shelley, *Frankenstein* (Mineola, NY: Dover, 1994), 151.

[10]Adoniram Judson uttered these inspiring words when he was hanging upside down and naked while being persecuted for his faith. Courtney Anderson, *To the Golden Shore* (Valley Forge, PA: Judson Press, 1988).